THE PERIODIC TABLE

KINGFISHER
NEW YORK

THE PERIODIC TABLE

ELEMENTS WITH STYLE!

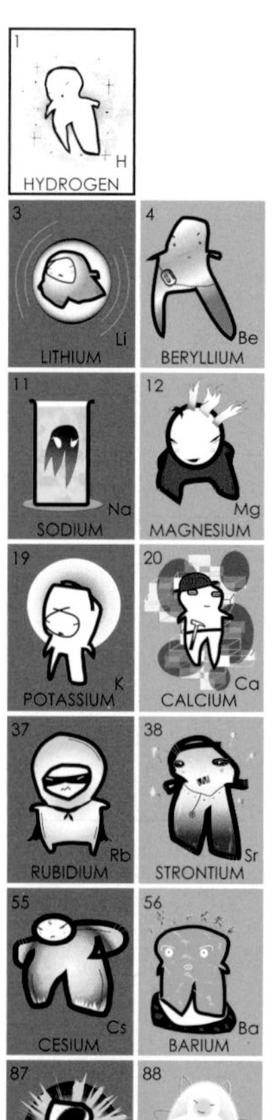

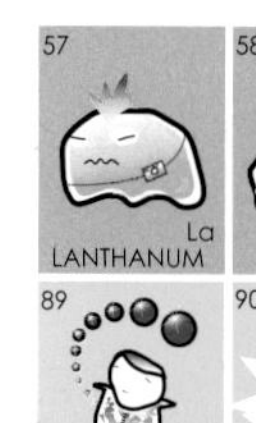

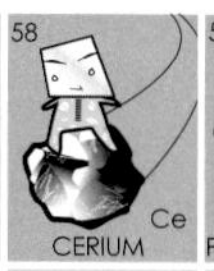

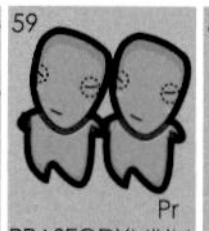

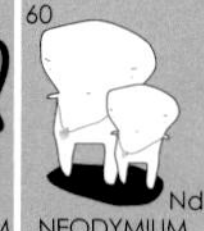

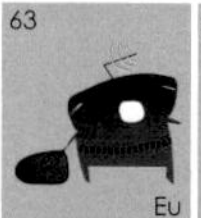

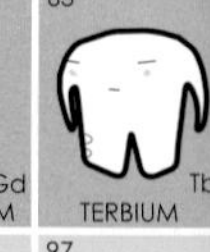

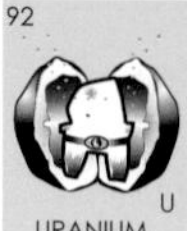

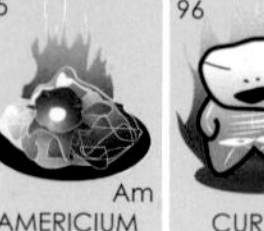

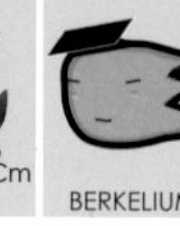

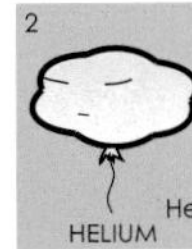
2
He
HELIUM

5 B BORON
6 C CARBON
7 N NITROGEN
8 O OXYGEN
9 F FLUORINE
10 Ne NEON
13 Al ALUMINUM
14 Si SILICON
15 P PHOSPHORUS
16 S SULFUR
17 Cl CHLORINE
18 Ar ARGON
30 Zn ZINC
31 Ga GALLIUM
32 Ge GERMANIUM
33 As ARSENIC
34 Se SELENIUM
35 Br BROMINE
36 Kr KRYPTON
48 Cd CADMIUM
49 In INDIUM
50 Sn TIN
51 Sb ANTIMONY
52 Te TELLURIUM
53 I IODINE
54 Xe XENON
80 Hg MERCURY
81 Tl THALLIUM
82 Pb LEAD
83 Bi BISMUTH
84 Po POLONIUM
85 At ASTATINE
86 Rn RADON
112 Cn COPERNICIUM
113 Uut ELEMENT 113
114 FL FLEROVIUM
115 Uup ELEMENT 115
116 Lv LIVERMORIUM
117 Uus ELEMENT 117
118 Uuo ELEMENT 118

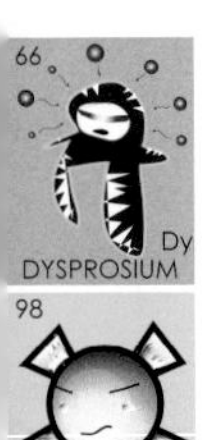
66 Dy DYSPROSIUM
98 Cf CALIFORNIUM

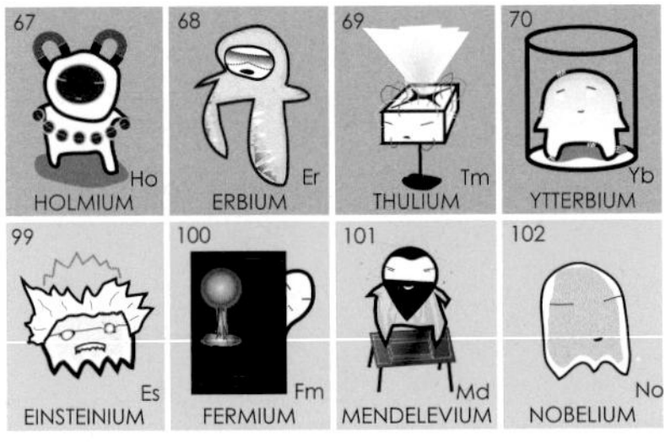
67 Ho HOLMIUM
68 Er ERBIUM
69 Tm THULIUM
70 Yb YTTERBIUM
99 Es EINSTEINIUM
100 Fm FERMIUM
101 Md MENDELEVIUM
102 No NOBELIUM

KINGFISHER
NEW YORK

Published in the United States by Kingfisher,
175 Fifth Ave., New York, NY 10010
Kingfisher is an imprint of Macmillan Children's Books, London.

Science Consultant: Dr. Christopher Hutchinson
Consultant: Dr. Mark Winter
Dr. Winter is a senior lecturer of chemistry at the University of Sheffield, England, and the author of www.webelements.com.
This book uses data adapted from www.webelements.com.

Designed and created by Basher
www.basherbooks.com

Dedicated to Ella Marbrook

Distributed in the U.S. and Canada by Macmillan, 175 Fifth Ave., New York, NY 10010

Library of Congress Cataloging-in-Publication Data
Dingle, Adrian.
The periodic table/Adrian Dingle.—1st ed.
p. cm.
Includes index.
ISBN-13: 978-0-7534-6085-6
1. Periodic law—Tables—Juvenile literature. 2.Chemical elements—Juvenile literature. I. Title.
QD467.D56 2007
546'.8—dc22
2006022515

ISBN: 978-0-7534-6085-6

Kingfisher books are available for special promotions and premiums.
For details contact: Special Markets Department, Macmillan,
175 Fifth Avenue, New York, NY 10010.

For more information, please visit www.kingfisherbooks.com

Printed in China
17
17TR/0116/WKT/SC/128MA

CONTENTS

The Periodic Table

Introduction

Everything in the world is made of elements—substances that cannot be broken down or made into anything simpler by chemical reactions. Each element has its own unique personality. Many, such as gold, silver, and lead, have been known for thousands of years. Others, such as livermorium, have been created in high-tech labs only as recently as 2000, and chemists have been busy making more.

The periodic table was the brainchild of Siberian superchemist Dmitri Mendeleev. In 1869, he arranged the known elements into groups (columns) and periods (rows), leaving gaps in his table for chemical elements that were still undiscovered at the time. Today the gaps have been filled, and there are a total of 111 known elements, but there may be others that are yet undiscovered. The vertical groups of the table make up "families"—all closely related and liking the same sorts of chemical shenanigans. In this book you'll meet the most representative characters from each group, as well as the breakaways and mavericks that do things their own way. . . .

101 Md

Mendelevium (named after Mendeleev)

1 Hydrogen

- Symbol: H
- Atomic number: 1
- Atomic weight: 1.0079
- Color: None
- Standard state: Gas at 25°C (77°F)
- Classification: Nonmetallic

I may be undersized, but don't underestimate me. I'm a petite package that packs a punch, and I have a fiery character to boot—always remember that I'm numero uno! I am the simplest and lightest of all the elements, the most abundant in the universe, and the source of everything in it—from matter and energy to life. I'm what powers nuclear fusion in the stars, and I'm the building block for all of the other elements of the periodic table.

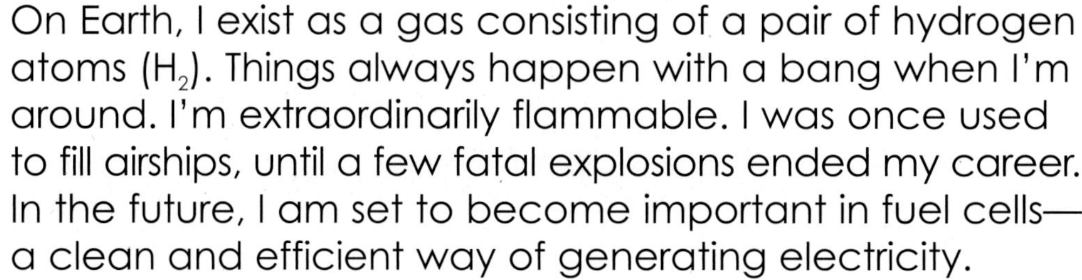

On Earth, I exist as a gas consisting of a pair of hydrogen atoms (H_2). Things always happen with a bang when I'm around. I'm extraordinarily flammable. I was once used to fill airships, until a few fatal explosions ended my career. In the future, I am set to become important in fuel cells—a clean and efficient way of generating electricity.

Date of discovery: 1766

- Density 0.082 g/l
- Melting point −259.14°C (−434.45°F)
- Boiling point −252.87°C (−423.17°F)

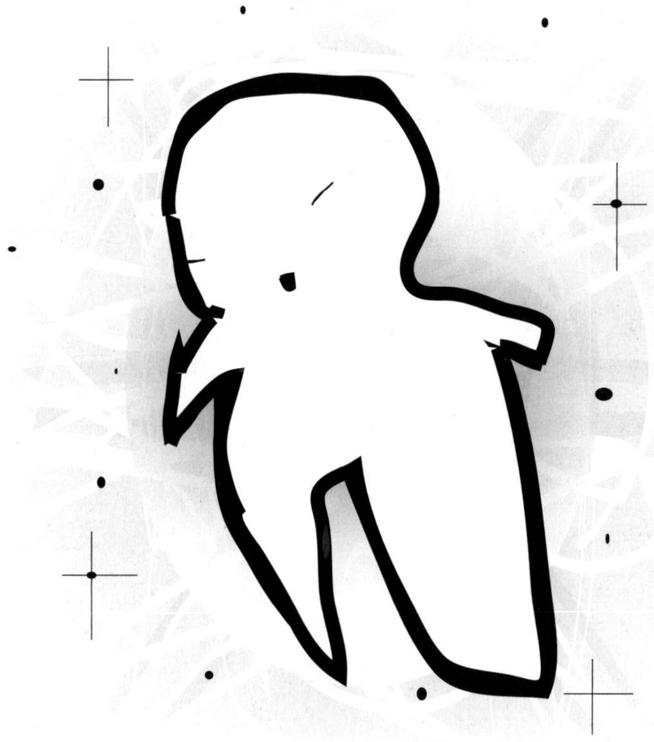

H

Hydrogen

CHAPTER 1

The Alkali Metals

Group 1

A rowdy bunch of rebels, these elements have a reputation for extremely reactive behavior. Chemically too feisty to be found unchanged in nature, this group is closer and more alike than any other group of the periodic table. All members are low-density, soft metals. When added to water, they turn it alkaline. Their dangerous desperation to lose their outer electron increases with their atomic number, and as soon as they come into contact with almost anything (including air), a violently explosive reaction follows. . . .

3
Li
LITHIUM

11
Na
SODIUM

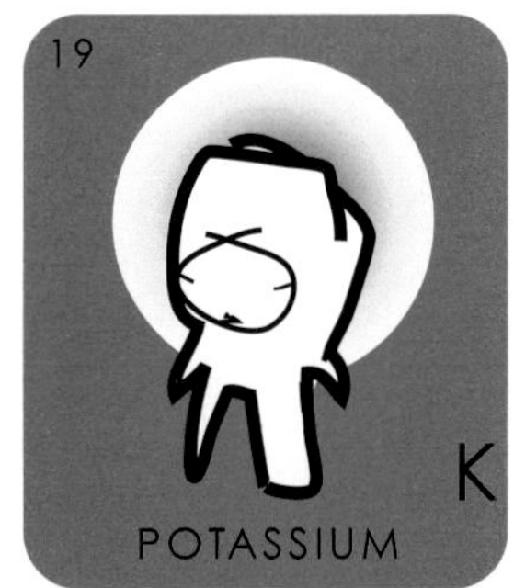
19
K
POTASSIUM

37
Rb
RUBIDIUM

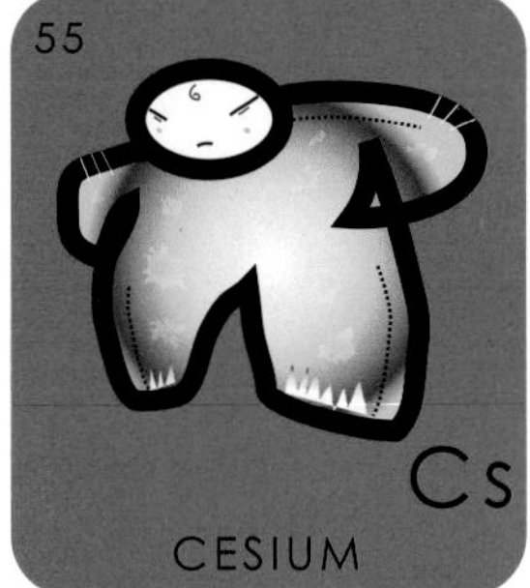
55
Cs
CESIUM

87
Fr
FRANCIUM

3 Lithium

The Alkali Metals

- Symbol: Li
- Atomic number: 3
- Atomic weight: 6.941
- Color: Silvery gray/white
- Standard state: Solid at 25°C (77°F)
- Classification: Metallic

The lightest of all metals on the periodic table and the first, I am a real soft touch. You can easily slice me with a knife, but when I'm combined with other metals like aluminum, I make very strong (and light) alloys. These qualities make me popular with the aerospace industry.

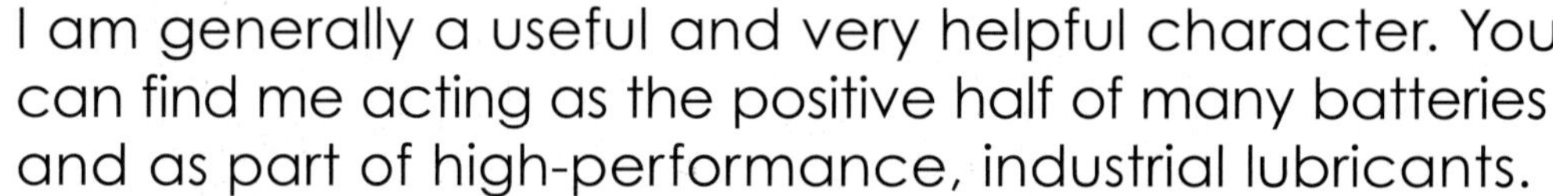

I am generally a useful and very helpful character. You can find me acting as the positive half of many batteries and as part of high-performance, industrial lubricants.

As lithium chloride (me plus chlorine), I'm remarkably good at absorbing large amounts of water. Taken as lithium carbonate (me, oxygen, and carbon), I help restore damaged personalities—calming and relieving sufferers of mental illnesses such as bipolar disorder.

Date of discovery: 1817

- Density 0.535 g/cm^3
- Melting point 180.54°C (356.97°F)
- Boiling point 1,342°C (2,447.6°F)

Lithium

11 Sodium

The Alkali Metals

- Symbol: Na
- Atomic number: 11
- Atomic weight: 22.99
- Color: Gray/white
- Standard state: Solid at 25°C (77°F)
- Classification: Metallic

I'm a complete live wire—high-strung and volatile—but I get along well with everyone and make strong, long-lasting friendships. I'm a gray-colored metal that's soft enough to be cut with a knife. I'm really reactive—you need to store me under oil to stop me from chemically reacting with the oxygen in air, and I'll explode into flames on contact with water!

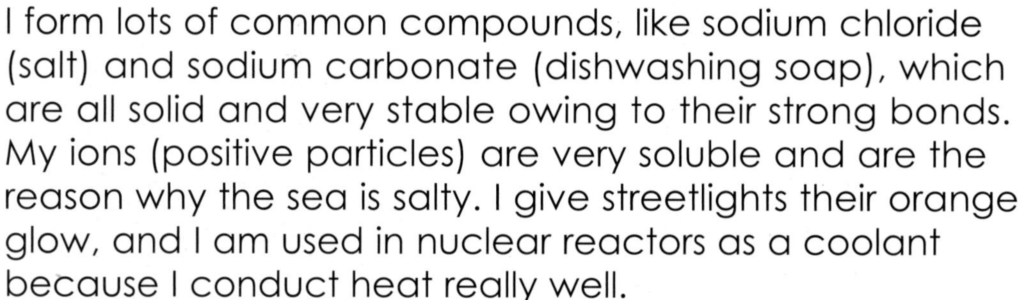

I form lots of common compounds, like sodium chloride (salt) and sodium carbonate (dishwashing soap), which are all solid and very stable owing to their strong bonds. My ions (positive particles) are very soluble and are the reason why the sea is salty. I give streetlights their orange glow, and I am used in nuclear reactors as a coolant because I conduct heat really well.

Date of discovery: 1807

- Density 0.968 g/cm^3
- Melting point 97.72°C (207.9°F)
- Boiling point 883°C (1,621.4°F)

Sodium

19 **Potassium**

The Alkali Metals

- Symbol: K
- Atomic number: 19
- Atomic weight: 39.098
- Color: Silver
- Standard state: Solid at 25°C (77°F)
- Classification: Metallic

I am sodium's twin. I am soft and react with air, so storing me under oil is essential. This small precaution keeps me isolated from contact with air or water. My ions can be easily detected in any substance since they give off a bright lilac flame. Just as dazzling is my explosive reaction with water, which is even stronger than that of sodium.

Everyone knows that I can be found in bananas, but I bet you didn't know that I am central to many processes in your body. Most vitally, I aid the function of the nerves, allowing the brain to transmit information to the muscles. But too much of me in the body can lead to a heart attack, and this is my darker side—in the U.S., potassium chloride is used in the lethal injections that kill Death Row prisoners.

Date of discovery: 1807

- Density 0.856 g/cm^3
- Melting point 63.38°C (146.08°F)
- Boiling point 759°C (1,398.2°F)

K

Potassium

37 **Rubidium**

■ The Alkali Metals

- Symbol: Rb
- Atomic number: 37
- Atomic weight: 85.468
- Color: Silvery
- Standard state: Solid at 25°C (77°F)
- Classification: Metallic

I'm scarce and hard to find. If you do unearth me, you'll see that I am a master of disguise and can mimic my cousins in Group 1. Like the rest of the gang, I'm superreactive. I go off with a bang on contact with air or water. Since I'm such a rare prankster, I'm very expensive. Watch out for future medicinal uses. . . .

Date of discovery: 1861

Rb

- Density 1.532 g/cm^3
- Melting point 39.31°C (102.76°F)
- Boiling point 688°C (1,270.4°F)

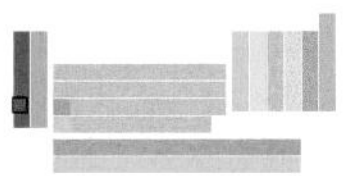

Cesium 55

The Alkali Metals

- Symbol: Cs
- Atomic number: 55
- Atomic weight: 132.91
- Color: Golden tinge
- Standard state: Solid at 25°C (77°F)
- Classification: Metallic

Soft and golden, I'm way more exciting than gold. When provoked, I give off a sky-blue light. Of my Group 1 gang, I have the fiercest reaction to water. I keep the beat in atomic clocks—accurate to one second every several hundred thousand years! My nasty radioactive isotope, cesium-137, was a major pollutant after the 1986 Chernobyl nuclear disaster in the former U.S.S.R.

- Density 1.879 g/cm^3
- Melting point 28.44°C (83.19°F)
- Boiling point 671°C (1,239.8°F)

Date of discovery: 1860

CHAPTER 2

The Alkaline Earth Metals

Group 2

The "alkaline earths" were once thought to be totally harmless and boring, because they were always found tightly bonded to oxygen. However, once released from these stable compounds, they began to act in the same unruly fashion as their next-door neighbors, the Group 1 family. Another gang of soft metals, these guys react easily and burn fiercely, getting meaner toward the base of the group. All are eager to lose their outer electrons, but this happens less easily than it does for the alkali metals, so they are a little less reactive.

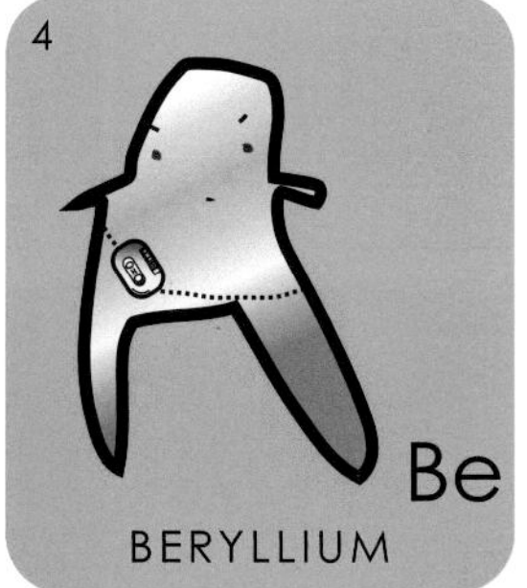
4
Be
BERYLLIUM

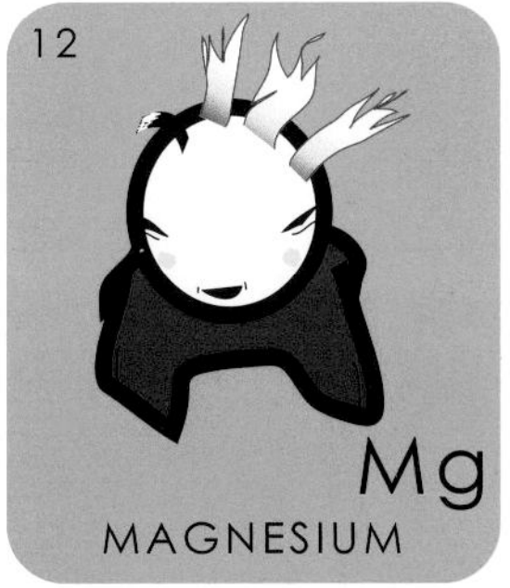
12
Mg
MAGNESIUM

20
Ca
CALCIUM

38
Sr
STRONTIUM

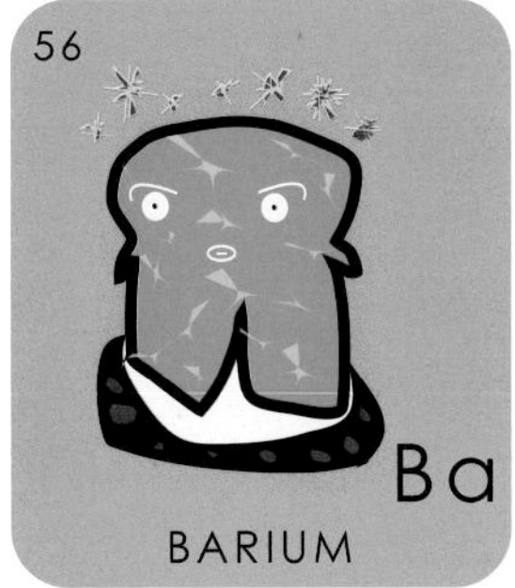
56
Ba
BARIUM

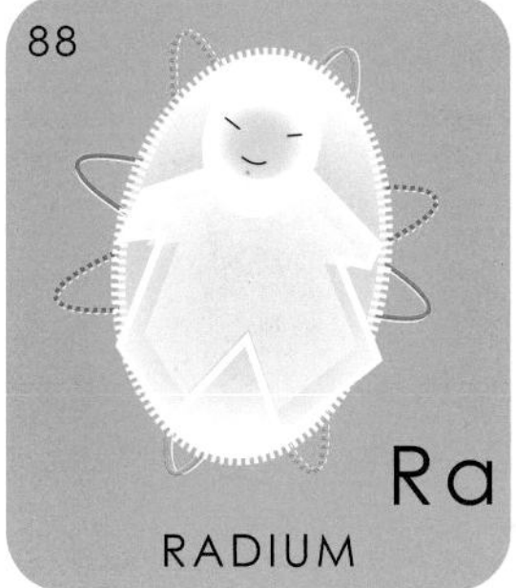
88
Ra
RADIUM

4 Beryllium

The Alkaline Earth Metals

- Symbol: Be
- Atomic number: 4
- Atomic weight: 9.0122
- Color: Silvery
- Standard state: Solid at 25°C (77°F)
- Classification: Metallic

Lucky for you, I am shy and secretive and don't get out much. A small amount of me in your body can give you berylliosis, a disease that inflames the lungs and is linked to lung cancer. As a metal, I am soft and silvery, and I'm used mostly in metal alloys, in league with other metals. I make an excellent electrical conductor, and I'm very flexible, too. Because I am so superlight, I also get used in the manufacture of airplanes.

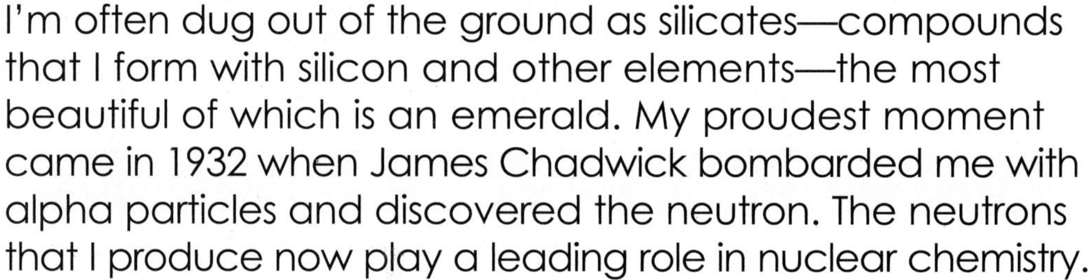

I'm often dug out of the ground as silicates—compounds that I form with silicon and other elements—the most beautiful of which is an emerald. My proudest moment came in 1932 when James Chadwick bombarded me with alpha particles and discovered the neutron. The neutrons that I produce now play a leading role in nuclear chemistry.

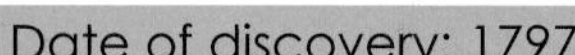

Date of discovery: 1797

Density	1.848 g/cm^3
Melting point	1,287°C (2,348.6°F)
Boiling point	2,469°C (4,476.2°F)

Be

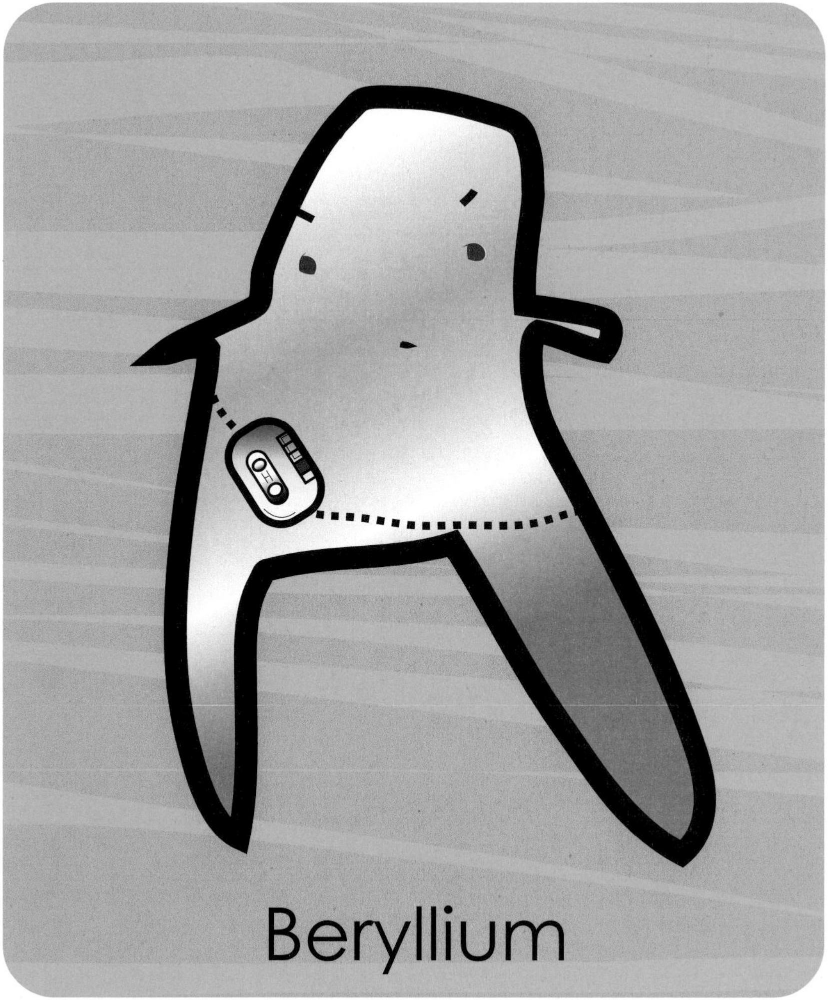

Beryllium

12 Magnesium

The Alkaline Earth Metals

- Symbol: Mg
- Atomic number: 12
- Atomic weight: 24.305
- Color: Silver-white
- Standard state: Solid at 25°C (77°F)
- Classification: Metallic

I'm happy to mix in any social gathering of the elements, making friends with anyone, even moody hydrogen. I'm sparky, and I always cause a reaction!

I'm a smart aleck, too—I can speed up your body processes and make you rush to the bathroom! The laxatives Epsom salts and milk of magnesia are both made using my salts, which also give a bitter taste to food and can leave a bad taste in your mouth.

I am a silver-white metal and burn with incredible intensity and a bright white light. My splendiferous powers of combustion are used in flashbulbs, distress flares, fireworks, and incendiary bombs. Strong and light, I help make bike frames, car parts, and aircraft engines.

Date of discovery: 1755

- Density 1.738 g/cm^3
- Melting point 650°C (1,202°F)
- Boiling point 1,090°C (1,994°F)

Magnesium

20 Calcium

The Alkaline Earth Metals

- Symbol: Ca
- Atomic number: 20
- Atomic weight: 40.078
- Color: Silvery
- Standard state: Solid at 25°C (77°F)
- Classification: Metallic

They call me "The Scaffolder" because I make up a large portion of the parts that hold you together—your skeleton and teeth. I'm needed in large amounts as you grow, to build the calcium phosphate of your bones, and as you get older to keep your frame strong.

A reactive metal, I'm soft and silvery in appearance, but I'm a bit harder on the inside. When my ions dissolve in water, it becomes "hard"—detergents won't lather, soap forms a surface scum, and limescale develops on faucets.

I've been known for hundreds of years and am found in common compounds such as lime, cement, chalk, and limestone. All of these are white, have been used in construction, and also have the ability to neutralize acid.

Date of discovery: 1808

Density	1.550 g/cm^3
Melting point	842°C (1,547.6°F)
Boiling point	1,484°C (2,703.2°F)

Calcium

38 **Strontium**

The Alkaline Earth Metals

- Symbol: Sr
- Atomic number: 38
- Atomic weight: 87.62
- Color: Silvery
- Standard state: Solid at 25°C (77°F)
- Classification: Metallic

I'm Scottish, named after the town of Strontian where I was discovered. You may see me as a shy, run-of-the-mill, silver-colored metal, but I've got a few surprises up my sleeve. I'll catch your eye with the stunning crimson colors that I give to fireworks. Today my main use is as an additive in the glass of TV sets and computer monitors.

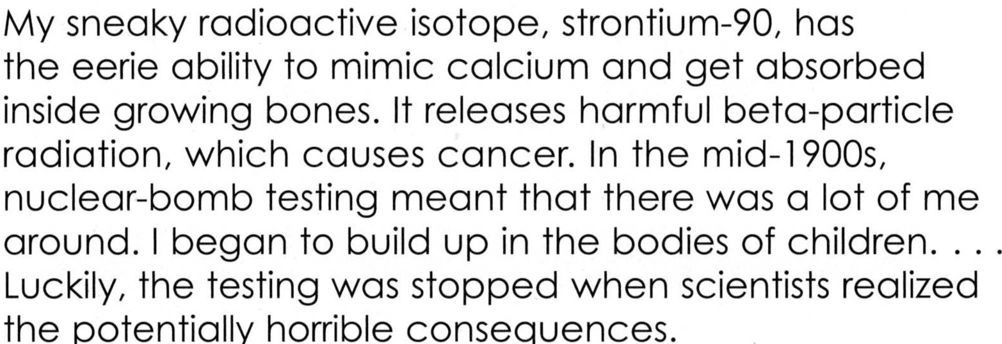

My sneaky radioactive isotope, strontium-90, has the eerie ability to mimic calcium and get absorbed inside growing bones. It releases harmful beta-particle radiation, which causes cancer. In the mid-1900s, nuclear-bomb testing meant that there was a lot of me around. I began to build up in the bodies of children. . . . Luckily, the testing was stopped when scientists realized the potentially horrible consequences.

Date of discovery: 1790

- Density 2.630 g/cm^3
- Melting point 777°C (1,430.6°F)
- Boiling point 1,382°C (2,519.6°F)

Strontium

56 **Barium**

The Alkaline Earth Metals

- Symbol: Ba
- Atomic number: 56
- Atomic weight: 137.33
- Color: Silver-white
- Standard state: Solid at 25°C (77°F)
- Classification: Metallic

One of the heavy metals, I'm a real rocker and more reactive than calcium. My carbonate salt is a deadly rat poison, but my sulfate salt is insoluble and totally indigestible. It's used for "barium meals," which are neither tasty nor nutritious, but are ideal for seeing how you are digesting your food. When excited, my ions give off an apple-green color.

Date of discovery: 1808

Ba

- Density 3.510 g/cm^3
- Melting point 727°C (1,340.6°F)
- Boiling point 1,870°C (3,398°F)

Radium 88

The Alkaline Earth Metals

- Symbol: Ra
- Atomic number: 88
- Atomic weight: 226.03
- Color: Silver-metallic
- Standard state: Solid at 25°C (77°F)
- Classification: Metallic

I am the heaviest of the gang and a completely captivating character.
I shine in any social situation. Bright and luminescent (I was used in glow-in-the-dark paint), I am a real stunner. I have the power to ionize air with the radioactive alpha particles that I give off, creating a crackling bright blue aura around me. My name comes from the Latin *radius*, meaning "ray."

Date of discovery: 1898

- Density 5.000 g/cm^3
- Melting point 700°C (1,292°F)
- Boiling point 1,737°C (3,158.6°F)

Ra

CHAPTER 3 The Transition Elements

Groups 3–12

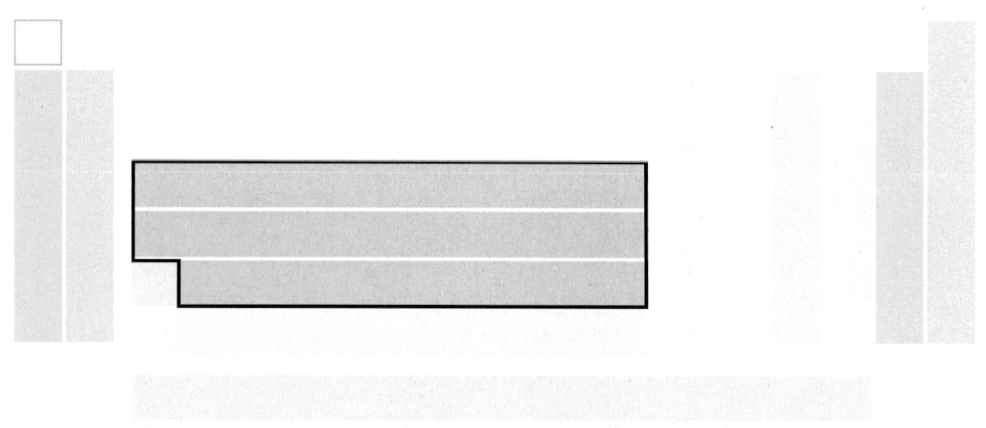

Stuck in the middle of the periodic table, the transition elements are a motley crew of roughnecks. Strapping, robust metals, these guys get involved in literally thousands of industrial applications. Many are movers and shakers that kick-start all sorts of important manufacturing reactions. Others use their amazing ability to bond with a wide variety of other elements to form alloys—some of which have changed civilization forever. But it's not all grit and grime: the transition elements love to show up in a dazzling variety of highly colored forms.

21 Sc SCANDIUM

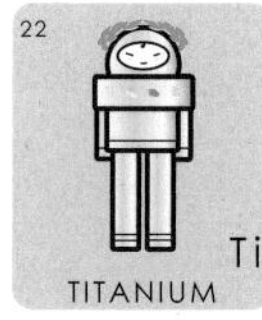
22 Ti TITANIUM

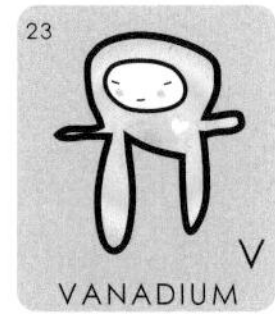
23 V VANADIUM

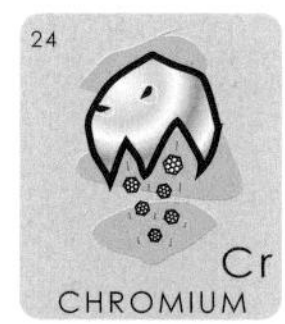
24 Cr CHROMIUM

25 Mn MANGANESE

26 Fe IRON

27 Co COBALT

28 Ni NICKEL

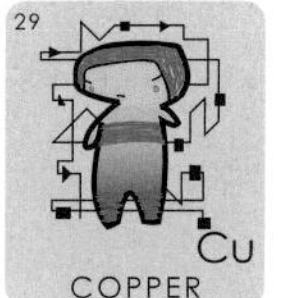
29 Cu COPPER

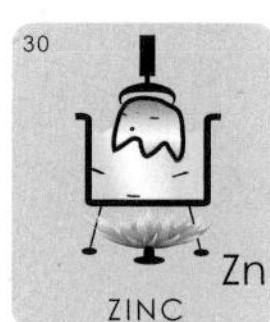
30 Zn ZINC

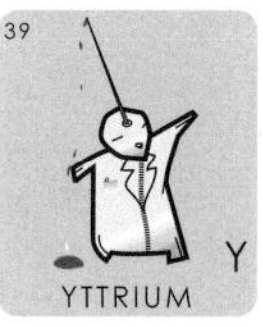
39 Y YTTRIUM

40 Zr ZIRCONIUM

41 Nb NIOBIUM

42 Mo MOLYBDENUM

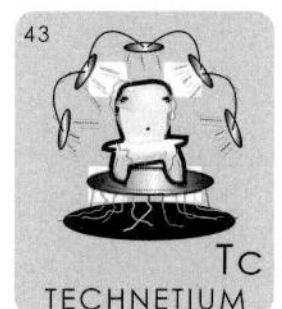
43 Tc TECHNETIUM

44 Ru RUTHENIUM

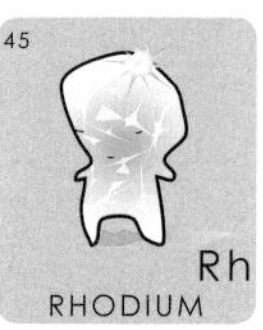
45 Rh RHODIUM

46 Pd PALLADIUM

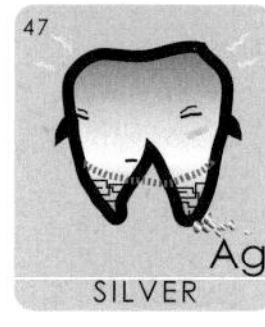
47 Ag SILVER

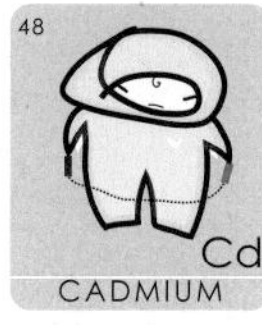
48 Cd CADMIUM

72 Hf HAFNIUM

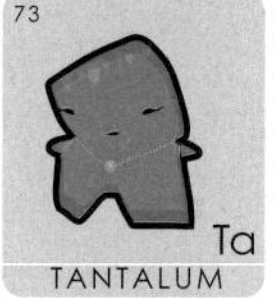
73 Ta TANTALUM

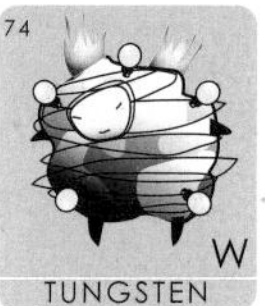
74 W TUNGSTEN

75 Re RHENIUM

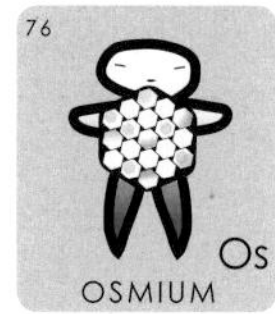
76 Os OSMIUM

77 Ir IRIDIUM

78 Pt PLATINUM

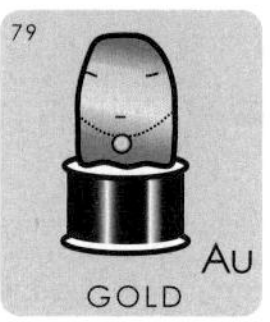
79 Au GOLD

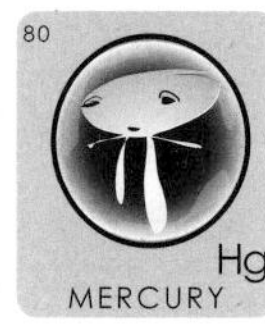
80 Hg MERCURY

22 Titanium

The Transition Elements

- Symbol: Ti
- Atomic number: 22
- Atomic weight: 47.867
- Color: Clean, gleaming silver
- Standard state: Solid at 25°C (77°F)
- Classification: Metallic

Titanium by name and a Titan by nature (Titans were strong, divine giants in Greek mythology), I am brilliant, gleaming, extremely hard, and very resistant to any type of chemical attacks.

As a dioxide compound (me plus two oxygen atoms), I'm bright white and excellent at spreading myself around. This combo makes me the king in the worlds of paint, paper, sunscreen, toothpaste, food dyes, and also in enameling and ceramic work.

My invulnerability makes me a favorite choice for bad-boy body piercings, but my main use is for superhard metal alloys. These are used in airplane and spacecraft manufacturing for their unrivaled combination of lightness and strength.

Date of discovery: 1791

- Density 4.507 g/cm^3
- Melting point 1,668°C (3,034.4°F)
- Boiling point 3,287°C (5,948.6°F)

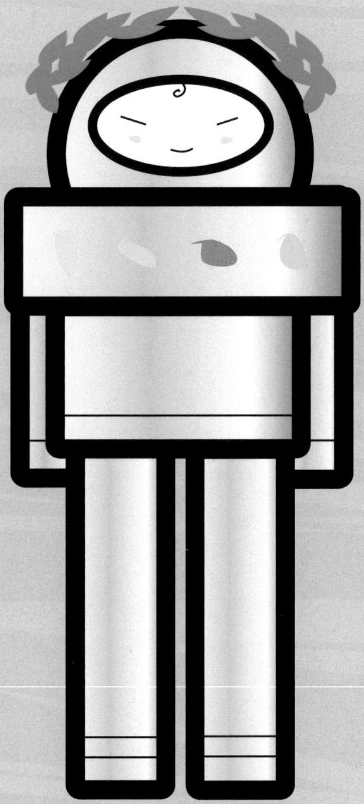

Ti

Titanium

23 Vanadium

The Transition Elements

- Symbol: V
- Atomic number: 23
- Atomic weight: 50.942
- Color: Silver-gray
- Standard state: Solid at 25°C (77°F)
- Classification: Metallic

My beauty knows no bounds. I am named after the Scandinavian goddess of beauty and love, Vanadis. Depending on my state (the charge of my various ions), I can make a rainbow of brilliant and beautiful purple, green, blue, and yellow solutions.

Like most transition metals, my colorful compounds can be used as catalysts (substances that allow chemical reactions to occur more freely). I am an essential catalyst in the "contact process" that is used to manufacture sulfuric acid, arguably the most important industrial chemical in the world today. I make up part of a crucial steel alloy that was used in Henry Ford's Model-T cars, so without me, there may never have been an auto industry.

Date of discovery: 1801

- Density 6.110 g/cm^3
- Melting point 1,910°C (3,470°F)
- Boiling point 3,407°C (6,164.6°F)

Vanadium

24 **Chromium**

The Transition Elements

- Symbol: Cr
- Atomic number: 24
- Atomic weight: 51.996
- Color: Supershiny silver
- Standard state: Solid at 25°C (77°F)
- Classification: Metallic

I'm totally flash. You may know me as a shiny, decorative metal on bikes and fancy kitchen equipment, but I am much more than just a pretty face. My name comes from the Greek word *chroma*, which means "color," because I can appear in an impressive range of funky shades (different oxidation states)—from red to green, orange, and yellow. I am responsible for the brilliant red color of rubies, and I put the "stainless" into stainless steel. There's no tarnishing my record!

It's easy to take a shine to me—just polish me with a cloth. I'm almost completely resistant to corrosion. Because of this, I was once used as a protective layer (a plating) to stop steel surfaces from rusting. I gave old cars their classic, mirrored-metal look. These days, most cars use plastic.

Date of discovery: 1797

Density	7.140 g/cm^3
Melting point	1,907°C (3,464.6°F)
Boiling point	2,671°C (4,839.8°F)

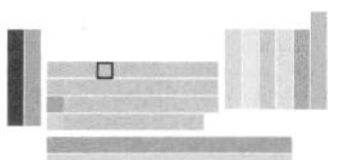

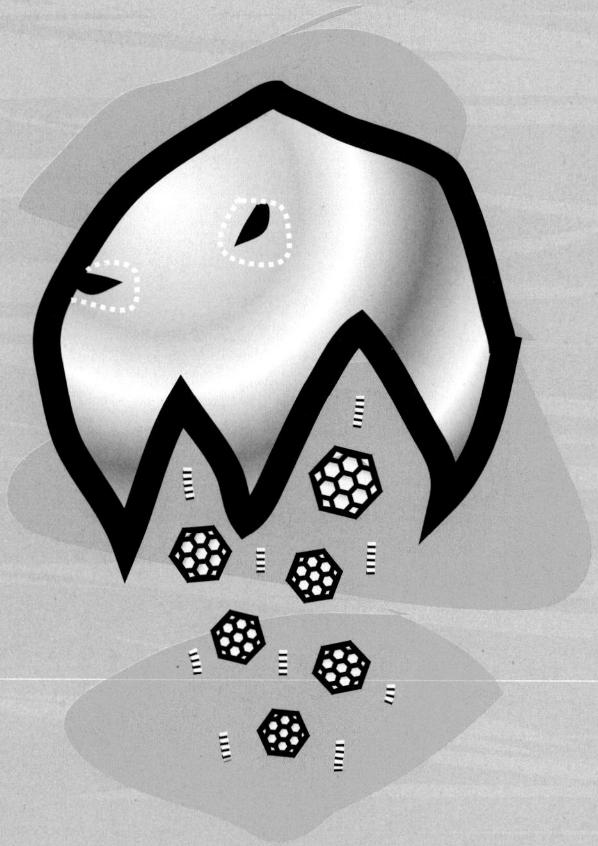

Chromium

25 Manganese

The Transition Elements

- Symbol: Mn
- Atomic number: 25
- Atomic weight: 54.938
- Color: Silvery
- Standard state: Solid at 25°C (77°F)
- Classification: Metallic

I'm a hard and brittle element. I am found in large amounts in the rocks of the ocean floor, and I'm most widely used in steel manufacturing. Steel is much stronger when it is joined with me in an alloy.

Like many of the other transition metals, I can exist in many different forms (oxidation states), and I change my appearance like an undercover agent—I can be pink, black, green, or dark purple.

Spend too long with me, and I'll mess with your mind. I play an important role in the body, but too much of me can give you "manganese madness," a terrifying psychiatric condition that causes hallucinations. I have also been associated with Parkinson's disease.

Date of discovery: 1774

- Density 7.470 g/cm^3
- Melting point 1,246°C (2,274.8°F)
- Boiling point 2,061°C (3,741.8°F)

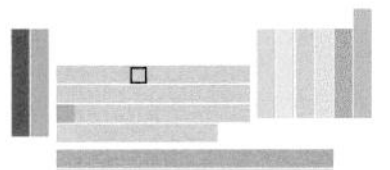

Mn

Manganese

26 Iron

The Transition Elements

- Symbol: Fe
- Atomic number: 26
- Atomic weight: 55.845
- Color: Gray
- Standard state: Solid at 25°C (77°F)
- Classification: Metallic

I am at the center of everything. I am the hub. As the main element in your blood's hemoglobin—the substance that transports oxygen throughout the body—I keep you alive. Journey to the center of Earth, and you'll find me there at the core of things. I am the most abundant element in the planet you live on, and I am at the heart of civilization, too.

I am the most important metal ever known to humankind. My use for tools and weapons transformed the ancient world; using me for construction and industrialization made the modern world. I'm most useful when I am mixed with small amounts of carbon to produce steel. But I'm not without flaws—I oxidize easily when exposed to air and water, making rust a constant problem.

Earliest known use: c. 2500 B.C.

Density	7.874 g/cm^3
Melting point	1,538°C (2,800.4°F)
Boiling point	2,861°C (5,181.8°F)

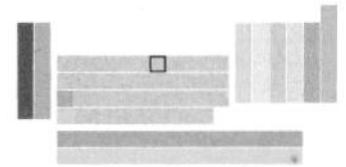

Iron

27 Cobalt

The Transition Elements

- Symbol: Co
- Atomic number: 27
- Atomic weight: 58.933
- Color: Gray
- Standard state: Solid at 25°C (77°F)
- Classification: Metallic

Mysterious and attractive, I am the gremlin of the underworld. My name was given to me by German miners, who called me *kobald*, meaning "goblin." They thought that I stopped them from getting to other more valuable metals, such as silver, and so believed that my beautiful ores had been cursed by goblins.

For hundreds of years, my compounds have been used to add my distinctive and attractive color to glass and objects. Although blue is my most well-known shade, green and pink are also prominent in my compounds.

My very useful radioactive isotope, cobalt-60, is a powerful gamma-ray emitter used for radiotherapy, leak detection in pipes, and irradiating food to kill bacteria.

Date of discovery: 1735

- Density 8.900 g/cm^3
- Melting point 1,495°C (2,723°F)
- Boiling point 2,927°C (5,300.6°F)

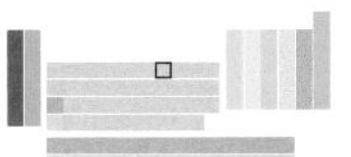

Co

Cobalt

28 Nickel

The Transition Elements

- Symbol: Ni
- Atomic number: 28
- Atomic weight: 58.693
- Color: Silvery
- Standard state: Solid at 25°C (77°F)
- Classification: Metallic

Some people think of me as the devil in disguise, because I'm often mistaken for copper. My name is taken from the German word *kupfernickel*, meaning "devil's copper." Unfair! I'm really likable and useful, too.

I love hanging out with the other transition metal elements, and I'm great at forming alloys that make materials stronger and more resistant to corrosion. You'll find me charging around batteries and in special heat-resistant materials. I am also used for plating car parts, as well as bathroom and kitchen fittings.

I make some exceptionally beautifully colored compounds, and my favorite shade is green. But this beauty is only skin-deep, and I can cause horrible rashes.

Date of discovery: 1751

Density	8.908 g/cm^3
Melting point	1,455°C (2,651°F)
Boiling point	2,913°C (5,275.4°F)

Nickel

29 Copper

The Transition Elements

- Symbol: Cu
- Atomic number: 29
- Atomic weight: 63.546
- Color: Reddish
- Standard state: Solid at 25°C (77°F)
- Classification: Metallic

I am an age-old metal that gave birth to whole chunks of history and launched civilizations. As a pure metal or mixed with tin to make bronze, I have been used for hundreds of years to make ornaments and practical tools. Along with tin, I formed the basis of the Bronze Age.

I am unique among metals in that I have a red hue, but some of my salts are a vivid blue. In fact, many sea creatures have blue blood because of my presence.

I'm the poor relation in a very well-to-do family. Along with silver and gold, we're known as the "coinage metals." However, these days I'm only used in very small amounts in pennies (along with zinc). I am an exceptional conductor of electricity and heat, so I'm also used in wiring.

Earliest known use: c. 4500 B.C.

- Density 8.920 g/cm^3
- Melting point 1,084.62°C (1,984.32°F)
- Boiling point 2,927°C (5,300.6°F)

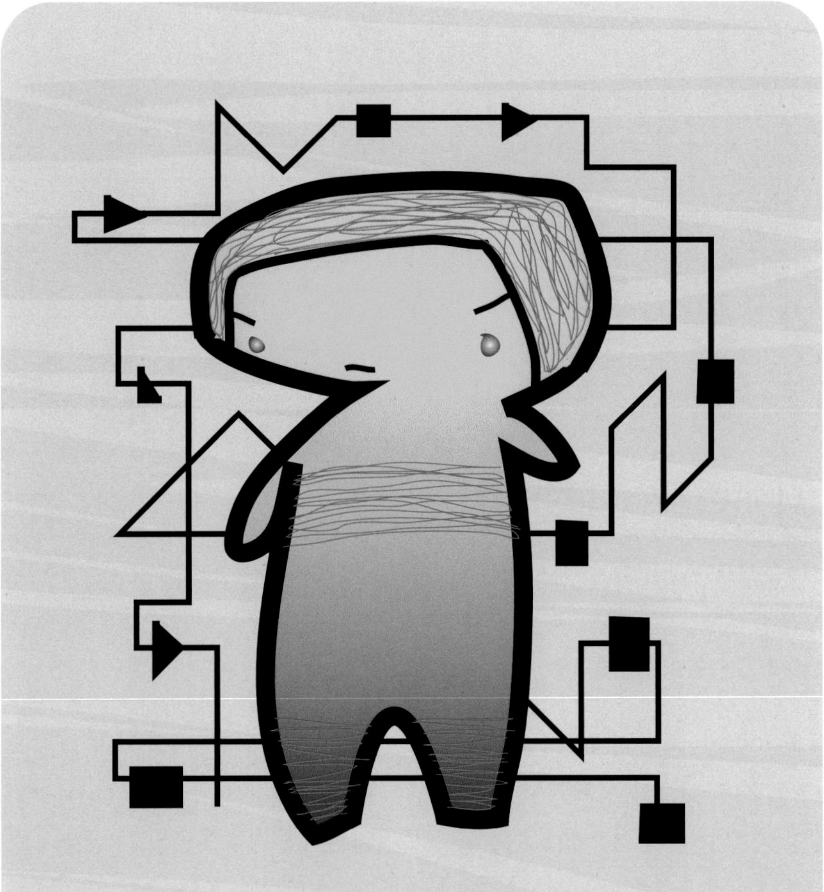

Copper

30 Zinc

The Transition Elements

- Symbol: Zn
- Atomic number: 30
- Atomic weight: 65.409
- Color: Bluish-gray
- Standard state: Solid at 25°C (77°F)
- Classification: Metallic

Here to protect and serve, I'm more useful than you'd ever zinc! I'm a very sociable element that's always happy to mix in with other metals. Brass is probably my most well-known alloy, formed when I get together with copper. On my own I can be found in batteries.

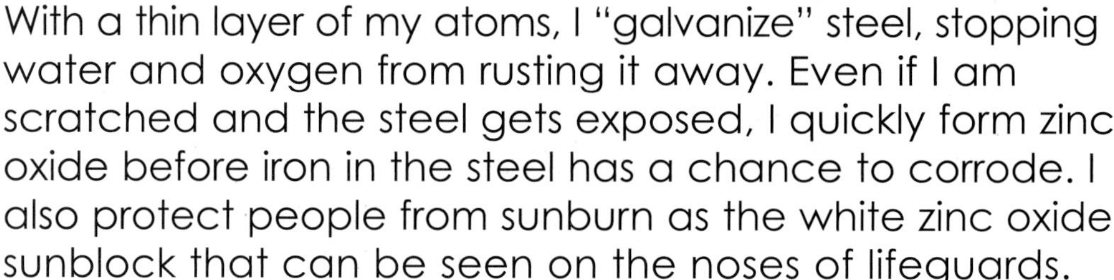

With a thin layer of my atoms, I "galvanize" steel, stopping water and oxygen from rusting it away. Even if I am scratched and the steel gets exposed, I quickly form zinc oxide before iron in the steel has a chance to corrode. I also protect people from sunburn as the white zinc oxide sunblock that can be seen on the noses of lifeguards.

What's more, I'm an essential element for lots of body processes, and I can be taken as a dietary supplement.

Date of discovery: 1500

Density	7.140 g/cm^3
Melting point	419.53°C (787.15°F)
Boiling point	907°C (1,664.6°F)

Zn

Zinc

42 **Molybdenum**

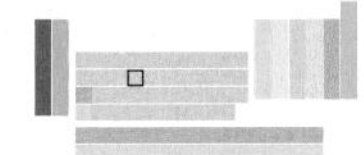

The Transition Elements

- Symbol: Mo
- Atomic number: 42
- Atomic weight: 95.94
- Color: Gray
- Standard state: Solid at 25°C (77°F)
- Classification: Metallic

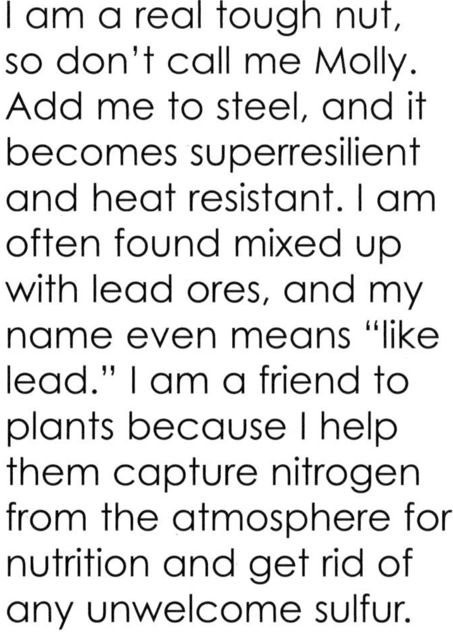

I am a real tough nut, so don't call me Molly. Add me to steel, and it becomes superresilient and heat resistant. I am often found mixed up with lead ores, and my name even means "like lead." I am a friend to plants because I help them capture nitrogen from the atmosphere for nutrition and get rid of any unwelcome sulfur.

Date of discovery: 1781

Mo

- Density 10.280 g/cm^3
- Melting point 2,623°C (4,753.4°F)
- Boiling point 4,639°C (8,382.2°F)

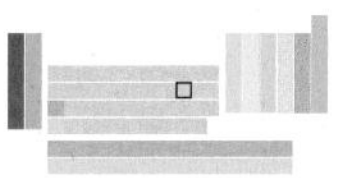

Palladium 46

The Transition Elements

- Symbol: Pd
- Atomic number: 46
- Atomic weight: 106.42
- Color: Silvery
- Standard state: Solid at 25°C (77°F)
- Classification: Metallic

I'm a wizard all around the industrial world because of my amazing skill as a catalyzer of reactions. This makes me even more sought after than my close cousin, platinum. The secret lies in my surface pores. Hard at work in the catalytic converters of modern cars, I can potentially save the planet from harmful hydrocarbon emissions.

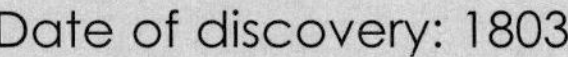

Date of discovery: 1803

- Density 12.023 g/cm^3
- Melting point 1,554.9°C (2,830.82°F)
- Boiling point 2,963°C (5,365.4°F)

Pd

47 **Silver**

The Transition Elements

- Symbol: Ag
- Atomic number: 47
- Atomic weight: 107.87
- Color: Silver
- Standard state: Solid at 25°C (77°F)
- Classification: Metallic

I'm as lustrous and luscious as a shining star! Whether made into money, jewelry, or candlesticks, I have always been coveted for my short-lived shininess. But I always lose out to gold because I can't help forming silver sulfide when I come into contact with air. This forms a layer of black tarnish that needs to be cleaned off.

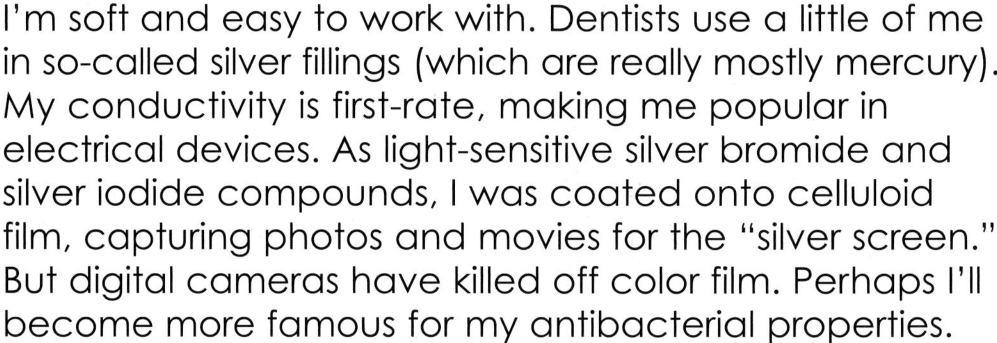

I'm soft and easy to work with. Dentists use a little of me in so-called silver fillings (which are really mostly mercury). My conductivity is first-rate, making me popular in electrical devices. As light-sensitive silver bromide and silver iodide compounds, I was coated onto celluloid film, capturing photos and movies for the "silver screen." But digital cameras have killed off color film. Perhaps I'll become more famous for my antibacterial properties.

Earliest known use: c. 3000 B.C.

Density	10.490 g/cm^3
Melting point	961.78°C (1,763.2°F)
Boiling point	2,162°C (3,923.6°F)

Silver

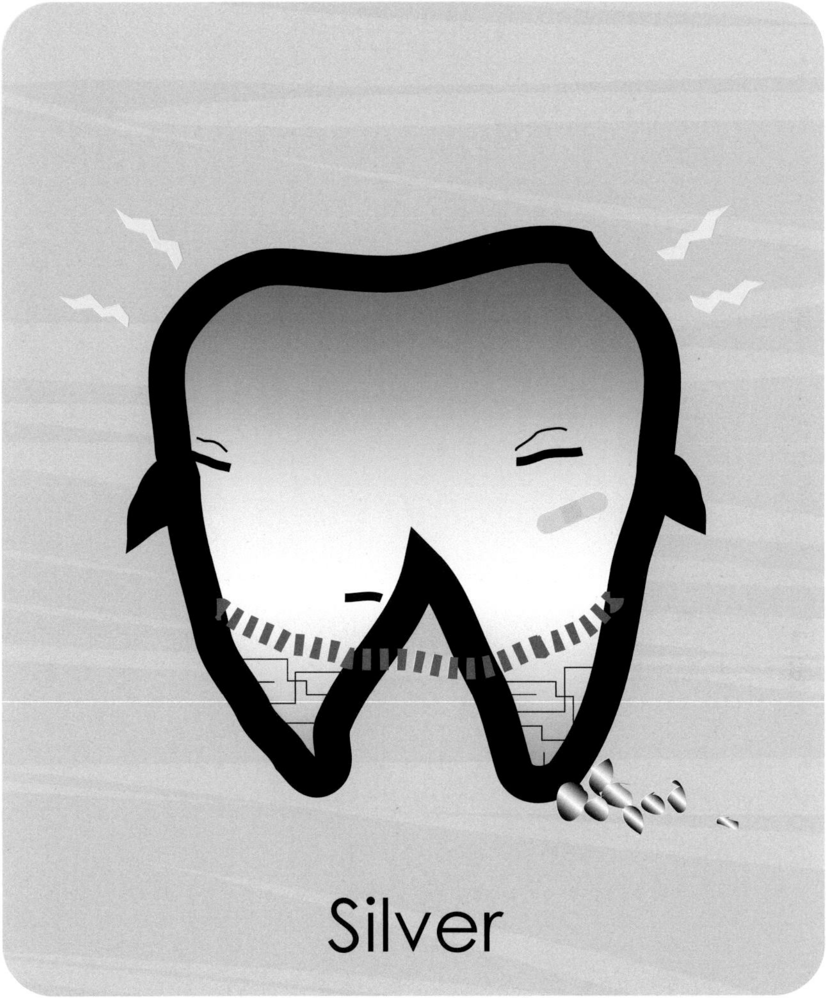

74 Tungsten

The Transition Elements

- Symbol: W
- Atomic number: 74
- Atomic weight: 183.84
- Color: Gray-white
- Standard state: Solid at 25°C (77°F)
- Classification: Metallic

Call me "Wolfram"—that's my old-school alter ego and the reason for my surprising chemical symbol. I'm one tough cookie, with the highest melting point of all metals and a boiling point close to 6,000°C (11,000°F), so you'll find me hard to liquefy and boil. In fact, you'll find me just plain harder than nails!

My compound tungsten carbide will tear through anything, like a knife through butter, so it's used to make high-speed cutting tools and drill bits. I am also used in golf clubs and balls and fishing weights (I'm more dense and much less toxic than lead). As the toughest of the tough, I can be found protecting soldiers as bulletproof armor plating, but I still manage to bring light to the world in the filaments of lightbulbs.

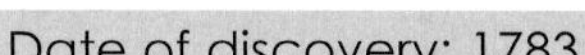

- Density 19.250 g/cm^3
- Melting point 3,422°C (6,196.6°F)
- Boiling point 5,555°C (10,031°F)

Tungsten

78 **Platinum**

The Transition Elements

- Symbol: Pt
- Atomic number: 78
- Atomic weight: 195.08
- Color: Silver-white
- Standard state: Solid at 25°C (77°F)
- Classification: Metallic

I'm the last word in good taste. Rarer and even more expensive than gold, I am a bright, shiny metal found in South Africa and Russia. I am a real ladies' metal, used to make jewelry and adored for my endlessly fascinating sheen. Steadfast and dependable, I never lose my shine because I'm resistant to corrosion.

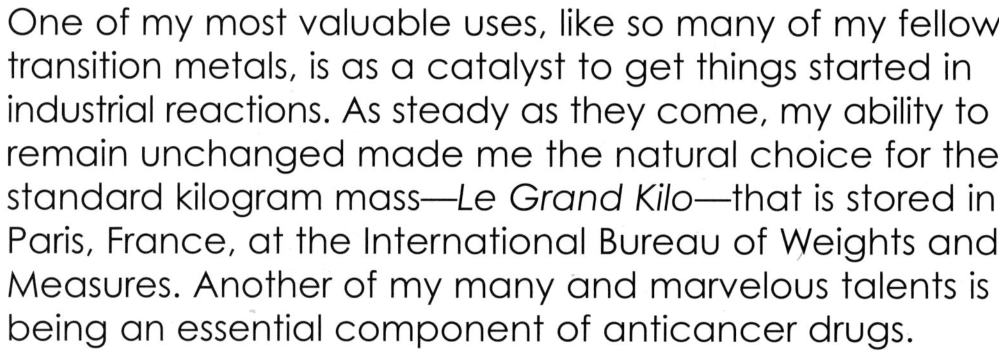

One of my most valuable uses, like so many of my fellow transition metals, is as a catalyst to get things started in industrial reactions. As steady as they come, my ability to remain unchanged made me the natural choice for the standard kilogram mass—*Le Grand Kilo*—that is stored in Paris, France, at the International Bureau of Weights and Measures. Another of my many and marvelous talents is being an essential component of anticancer drugs.

Date of discovery: 1735

Density	21.090 g/cm^3
Melting point	1,768.3°C (3,214.94°F)
Boiling point	3,825°C (6,917°F)

Platinum

79 **Gold**

The Transition Elements

- Symbol: Au
- Atomic number: 79
- Atomic weight: 196.97
- Color: Gold
- Standard state: Solid at 25°C (77°F)
- Classification: Metallic

I am not the rarest or the most expensive element, but I am the world's most wanted. I am the original gold-rush king, the ultimate attention seeker, and a bling party lover! At heart, I'm soft (for a metal), which makes me very easy to work with, and I can be polished to a high shine. My attraction lies in my resistance to corrosion (oxidation), meaning that I can be found in pure form inside Earth. I always remain a glistening temptation.

I am found in jewelry, in most electronic equipment (I'm a sparkling conductor of electricity), as crowns on teeth, in arthritis treatments, and, of course, as solid-gold bullion. My purity is measured in carats—24 carat is my purest form, but I can be alloyed (combined) with other metals to make 22-, 18-, 14- and nine-carat gold.

Earliest known use: c. 3000 B.C.

- Density 19.300 g/cm^3
- Melting point 1,064.18°C (1,947.52°F)
- Boiling point 2,856°C (5,172.8°F)

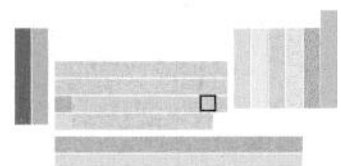

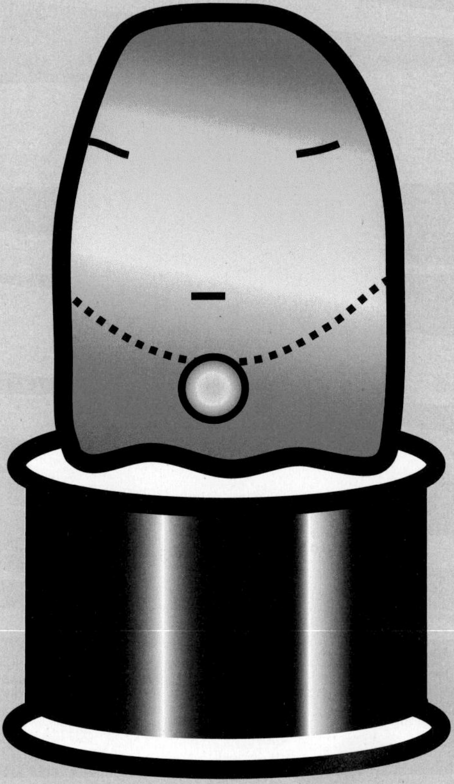

Gold

80 **Mercury**

The Transition Elements

- Symbol: Hg
- Atomic number: 80
- Atomic weight: 200.59
- Color: Silvery
- Standard state: Liquid at 25°C (77°F)
- Classification: Metallic

Quick and deadly, that's me. A sinister, silver-colored killer, I am a strange and stealthy liquid metal that easily vaporizes into toxic fumes. I put the "mad" in Mad Hatter—hat makers who used mercury nitrate for their work often succumbed to a strange delirium called "mercury madness." My ability to poison the brain is legendary, and most of the forms I take are lethal.

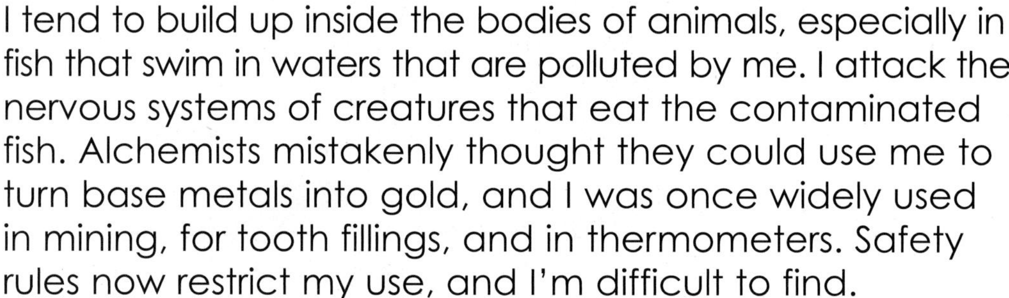

I tend to build up inside the bodies of animals, especially in fish that swim in waters that are polluted by me. I attack the nervous systems of creatures that eat the contaminated fish. Alchemists mistakenly thought they could use me to turn base metals into gold, and I was once widely used in mining, for tooth fillings, and in thermometers. Safety rules now restrict my use, and I'm difficult to find.

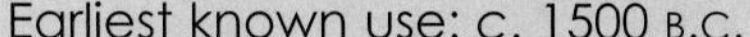

Earliest known use: c. 1500 B.C.

- Density: 13.534 g/cm^3
- Melting point: −38.83°C (−37.89°F)
- Boiling point: 356.73°C (674.11°F)

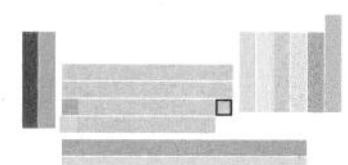

Mercury

CHAPTER 4

The Boron Elements

Group 13

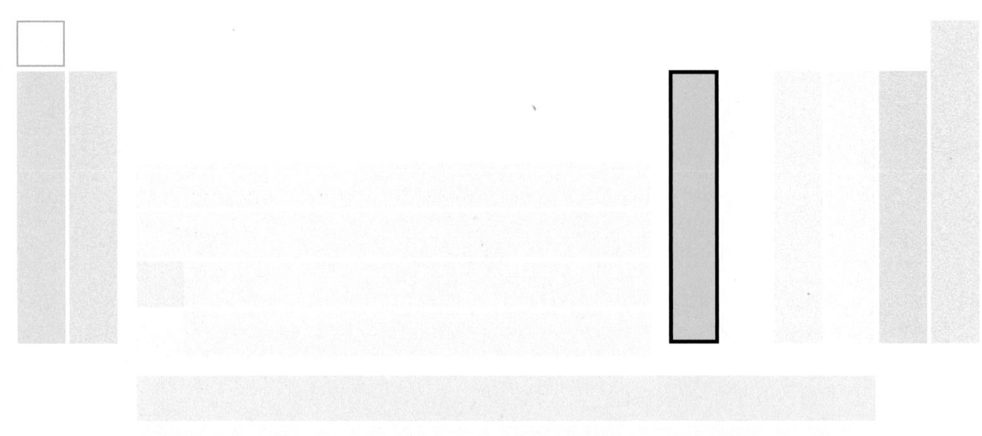

This ragtag group of elements is the periodic table's dysfunctional family. They don't gel together—some of them aren't even the same type of substance! Lonely, odd-man-out boron is an unusual powdery nonmetal, while the rest are soft, silvery, and weak metals. At the top of the group, these metals aren't especially metallic, but the farther down the group you go, the more like metals the members get. The boron elements are reactive enough to form many different compounds and are found in nature as various minerals and ores.

5
B
BORON

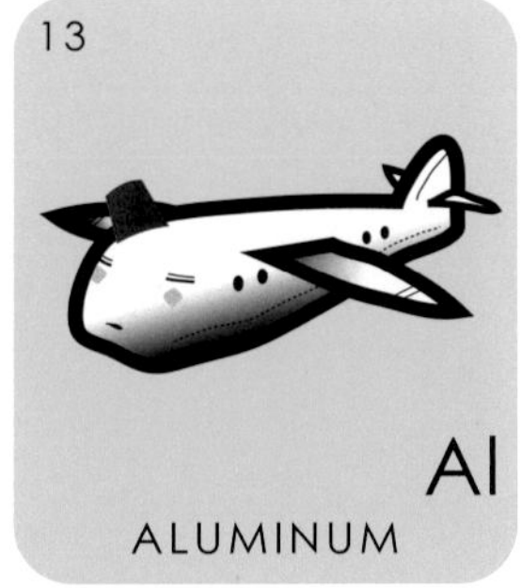
13
Al
ALUMINUM

31
Ga
GALLIUM

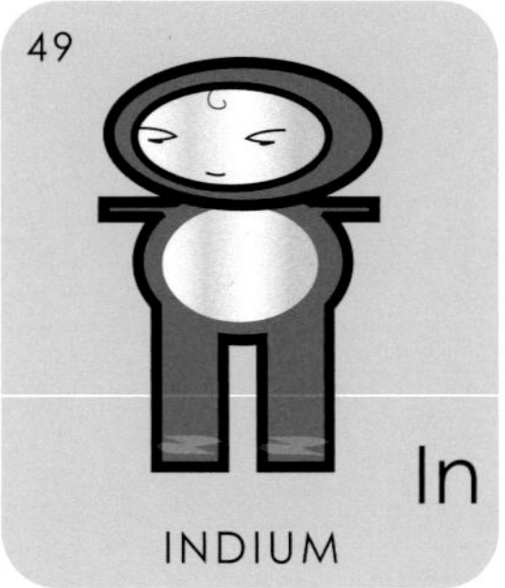
49
In
INDIUM

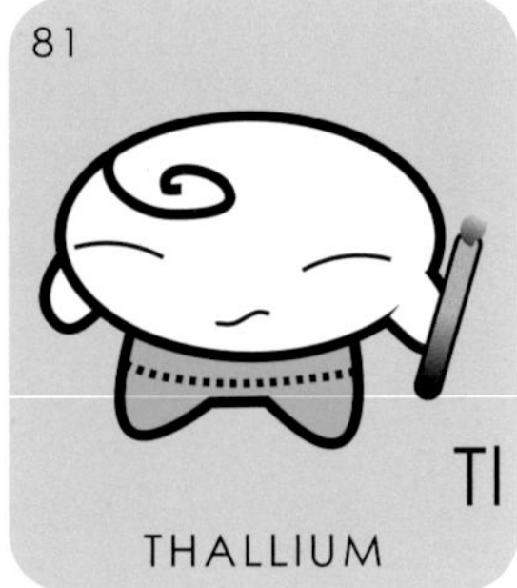
81
Tl
THALLIUM

113
Uut
ELEMENT 113

5 Boron

The Boron Elements

- Symbol: B
- Atomic number: 5
- Atomic weight: 10.811
- Color: Brownish-black
- Standard state: Solid at 25°C (77°F)
- Classification: Nonmetallic

People make fun of my name and call me "Boring Boron." Okay, so I'm not flamboyant and I dress in brown and black, but I'm really nice to have around. I'm a facilitator and a helpful element that gets things done—a self-starter, if I can be so bold.

Whether helping out in glass manufacturing, in detergents, or—in my guise as borax and boric acid—coaxing along chemical reactions in industry, I'm on the case. My compound boron nitrate is almost as hard as diamond.

Far from tedious, you can think of me as a maverick. I am literally the "black-brown sheep" of the boron element family, since I'm the only nonmetal among my metallic friends.

Date of discovery: 1808

- Density 2.460 g/cm^3
- Melting point 2,076°C (3,768.8°F)
- Boiling point 3,927°C (7,100.6°F)

B

Boron

13 **Aluminum**

The Boron Elements

- Symbol: Al
- Atomic number: 13
- Atomic weight: 26.982
- Color: Silver-gray
- Standard state: Solid at 25°C (77°F)
- Classification: Metallic

I'm light on my feet, and my pocket-battleship strength has made me a powerhouse metal. I am a featherweight who punches above my weight! I offer a superior blend of strength and lightness—you can make me into airplanes, "tin" cans, and foil.

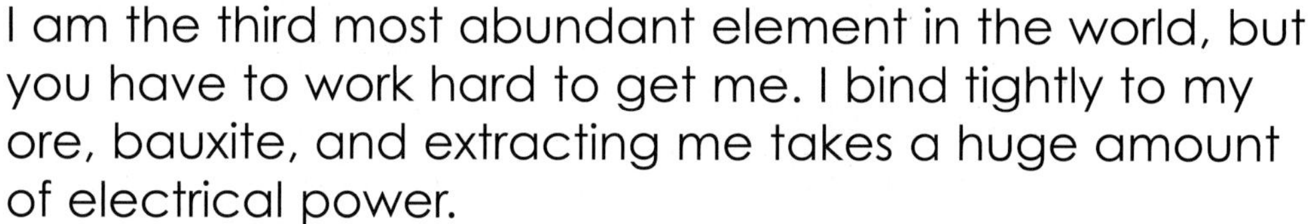

I am the third most abundant element in the world, but you have to work hard to get me. I bind tightly to my ore, bauxite, and extracting me takes a huge amount of electrical power.

My salts help purify water by causing impurities to drop out of solutions as solids, but they have been linked to poisoning. When I show up in tap water, I have turned people's hair green and caused brain disorders.

Date of discovery: 1825

- Density 2.700 g/cm^3
- Melting point 660.32°C (1,220.58°F)
- Boiling point 2,519°C (4,566.2°F)

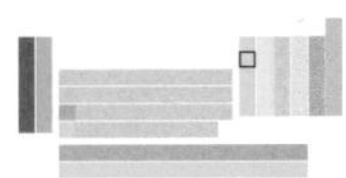

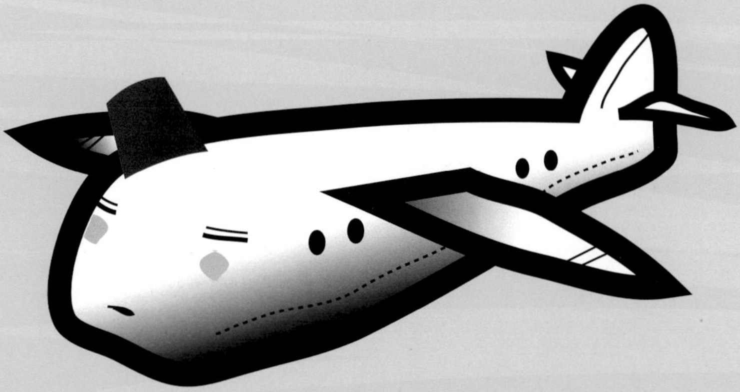

Aluminum

CHAPTER 5

The Carbon Elements

Group 14

Unpredictability hangs like a magician's cloak over this group of tricky chemicals. They have very few striking similarities. Carbon is a hard (and even sometimes transparent) nonmetal, while tin and lead are softer metals. Like Group 13, the carbon elements get more metallic toward the bottom of the table. The members form a bewildering variety of different compounds, so perhaps it would be better to consider each element as an individual, rather than as part of a collection of like-minded substances.

6
C
CARBON

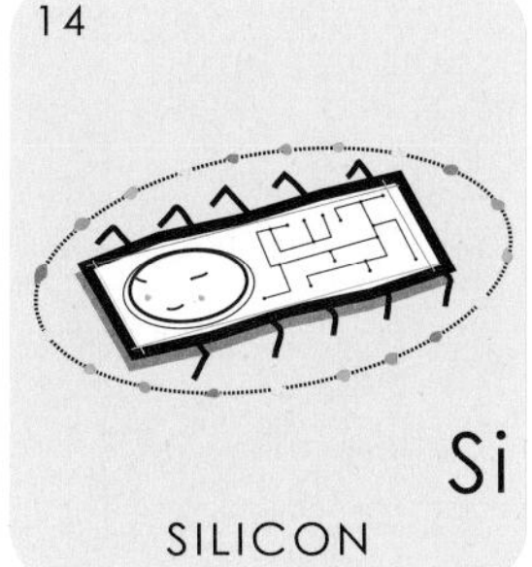
14
Si
SILICON

32
Ge
GERMANIUM

50
Sn
TIN

82
Pb
LEAD

114
Fl
FLEROVIUM

6 Carbon

The Carbon Elements

- Symbol: C
- Atomic number: 6
- Atomic weight: 12.011
- Color: Black
- Standard state: Solid at 25°C (77°F)
- Classification: Nonmetallic

Hah-yah! Wherever you look, I'm there. Like a ninja, there's no escaping me! A master of the black arts, I'm a stealthy element and can morph into many forms—black charcoal, hard and brilliant diamond, slippery graphite, wonder material graphene, and lovely buckminsterfullerene balls. My ability to form several types of chemical bonds with myself means that I can whip myself into all sorts of shapes. With so many different guises, there's a whole branch of "organic" chemistry devoted to me.

I form the bulk of all living matter. Almost everything you eat—fats, sugars, and fiber—is a carbon-based compound. I move around the food chain in what's called "the carbon cycle." I'm released from food when you breathe and in your body waste, absorbed by plants, and then eaten again.

No known date of discovery

- Density: 2.267 g/cm^3
- Melting point: 3,527°C (6,380.6°F)
- Boiling point: 4,027°C (7,280.6°F)

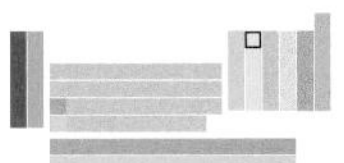

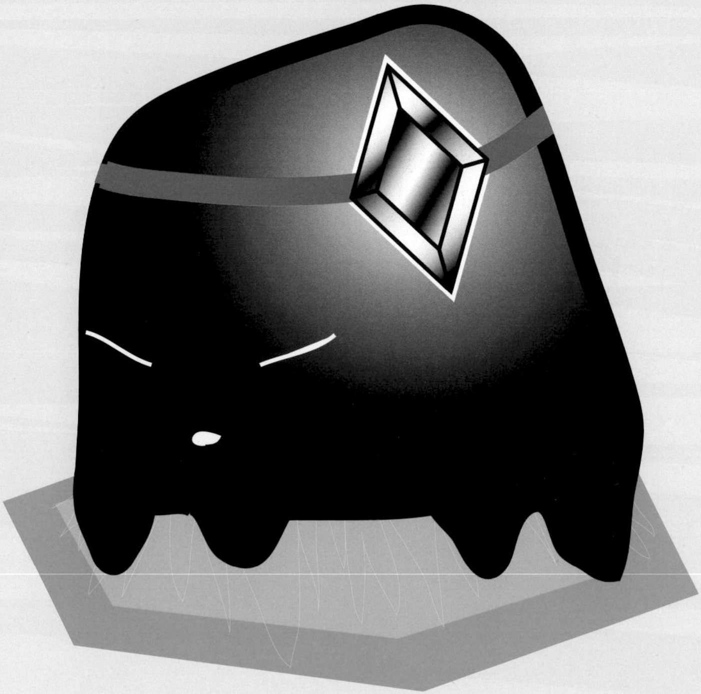

C

Carbon

14 Silicon

The Carbon Elements

- Symbol: Si
- Atomic number: 14
- Atomic weight: 28.086
- Color: Glassy off-white
- Standard state: Solid at 25°C (77°F)
- Classification: Nonmetallic

My beguiling charms make computers run and power the digital age. Combined with boron or phosphorus, I become a semiconducting sorcerer. These special powers gave birth to the silicon chip and the computer age. Silicon Valley in California is named after me.

I take many different forms. As the second most abundant element on Earth, I crop up in sand, quartz, flint, and countless other minerals. As the famous silicone (a long chain made up of me, oxygen, and organic chemicals), I'm in lubricants, adhesives, and body implants.

In glass, I'm perfectly clear. In quartz watches and clocks, I keep time, while as silica gel, I ensure that products are moisture-free. You'll find me inside sachets, packed inside boxes of electrical goods.

Date of discovery: 1824

- Density 2.330 g/cm^3
- Melting point 1,414°C (2,577.2°F)
- Boiling point 2,900°C (5,252°F)

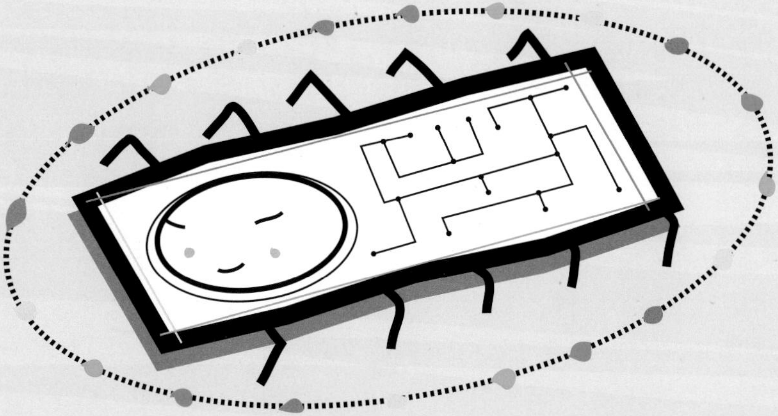

Silicon

50 Tin

The Carbon Elements

- Symbol: Sn
- Atomic number: 50
- Atomic weight: 118.71
- Color: Dull silver
- Standard state: Solid at 25°C (77°F)
- Classification: Metallic

I am a wily old metal with a long and distinguished history. Starting way back in the Bronze Age, I have been the ultimate mixer for metals. My most notable alloys are pewter (mingled with copper and bismuth), solder (teamed up with lead), and, of course, bronze (my ancient and long-lived partnership with copper).

I am too soft for my own good—in fact, I can be shaped with very little effort. But my problem is that I melt at a low temperature (for a metal), and below 13°C (55°F), I change from a solid into a crumbly powder. I get mixed with other metals to keep me in shape. (I'm only a thin coating on "tin" cans—they're actually made of aluminum or steel.) The "Pilkington process" produces pancake-flat glass by floating molten glass onto a surface of me in liquid form.

Earliest known use: c. 3500 B.C.

- Density 7.310 g/cm^3
- Melting point 231.93°C (449.47°F)
- Boiling point 2,602°C (4,715.6°F)

Sn

Tin

82 Lead

The Carbon Elements

- Symbol: Pb
- Atomic number: 82
- Atomic weight: 207.2
- Color: Dull, dark gray
- Standard state: Solid at 25°C (77°F)
- Classification: Metallic

Don't let my heavyweight status fool you—at heart I'm a completely malleable softy. I am so easy to work with that the ancient Romans used me for their water pipes. My chemical symbol (and the word "plumbing") comes from my Latin name, *plumbum*.

Over the years, I've gained a bad rep. People say that I build up in bones as a slow poison and that I have damaged childrens' development. It's true that I have an unfortunate ability to slip easily into the food chain—from pipes and cookware, leaded gasoline, and paints to fishermen's weights. I have also been blamed for ending the ancient Roman civilization. Not fair! These days, I am closely regulated. But I am still used as a shield against x-rays, for roofing, and in stained glass.

No known date of discovery

- Density 11.340 g/cm^3
- Melting point 327.46°C (621.43°F)
- Boiling point 1,749°C (3,180.2°F)

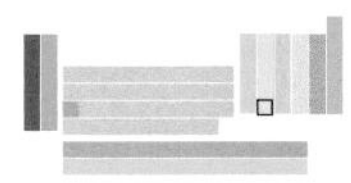

Pb

Lead

CHAPTER 6

The Nitrogen Elements

Group 15

The "pnictogens" (nick-toe-jens), as they are sometimes (but rarely) called, are an ancient and alchemical group with an odd collection of properties to boot. This group is a real mishmash of matter—there are metals, nonmetals, and strange metalloids; several elements exist in two different guises; and there's a mixture of gases and solids thrown in for good measure. Like most groups in the periodic table, the elements of Group 15 get increasingly metallic toward the base. Nitrogen is a colorless gas, while bismuth is a brittle metal.

7
N
NITROGEN

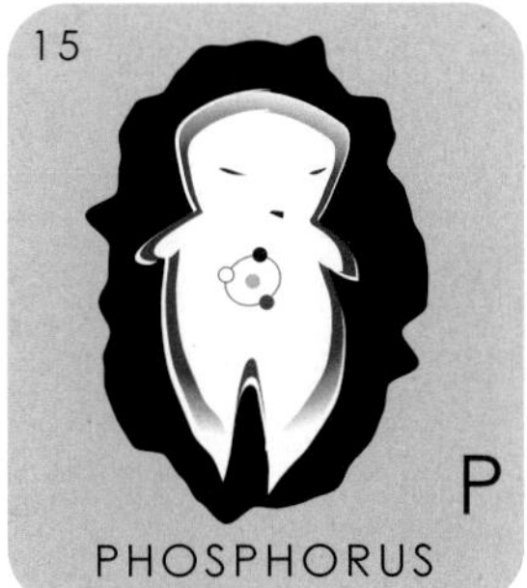
15
P
PHOSPHORUS

33
As
ARSENIC

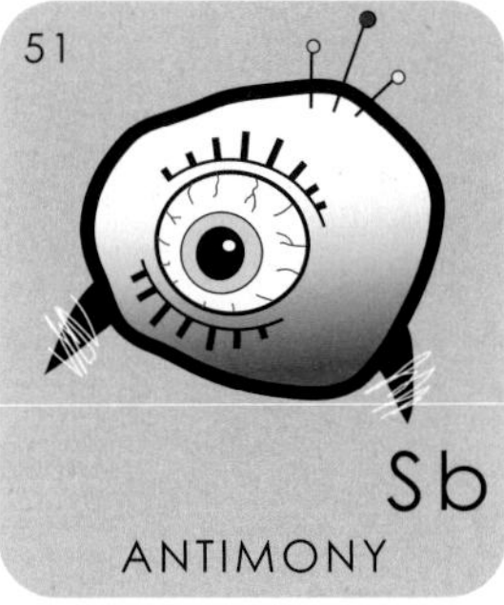
51
Sb
ANTIMONY

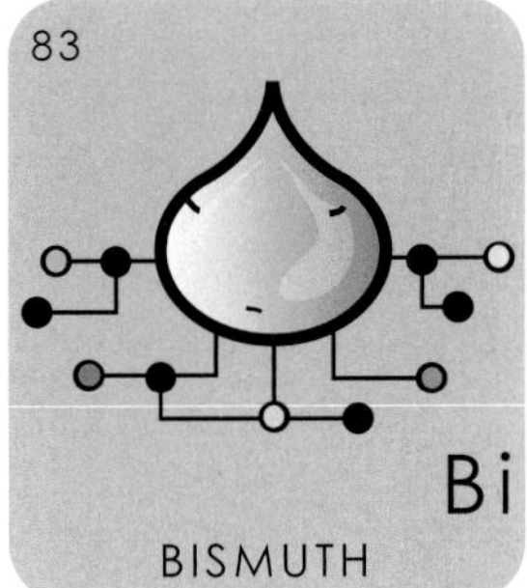
83
Bi
BISMUTH

115
Uup
ELEMENT 115

7 Nitrogen

The Nitrogen Elements

- Symbol: N
- Atomic number: 7
- Atomic weight: 14.007
- Color: None
- Standard state: Gas at 25°C (77°F)
- Classification: Nonmetallic

On first impression I'm a regular sort, but I've got an explosive temperament. You might hardly notice me, but I make up almost 80 percent of air, and I'm essential to plant life on Earth.

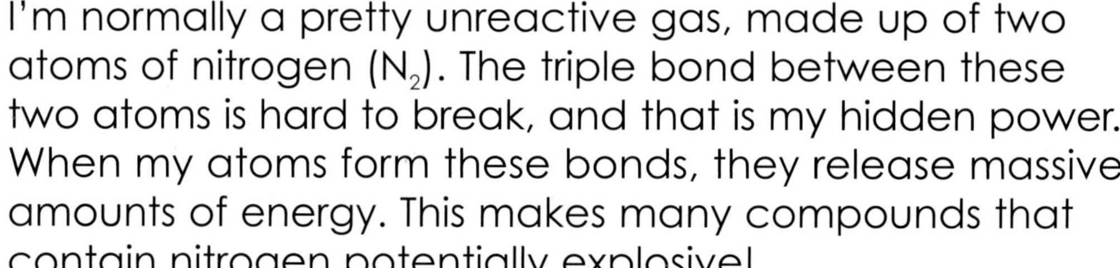

I'm normally a pretty unreactive gas, made up of two atoms of nitrogen (N_2). The triple bond between these two atoms is hard to break, and that is my hidden power. When my atoms form these bonds, they release massive amounts of energy. This makes many compounds that contain nitrogen potentially explosive!

I'm very easy to extract from air. I am a spectacular coolant in liquid form. At close to –200 °C (–328 °F), I will freeze almost anything that comes into contact with me.

Date of discovery: 1772

- Density 1.145 g/l
- Melting point –210.10°C (–346.18°F)
- Boiling point –195.79°C (–320.42°F)

Nitrogen

15 **Phosphorus**

The Nitrogen Elements

- Symbol: P
- Atomic number: 15
- Atomic weight: 30.974
- Color: Black, red, or white
- Standard state: Solid at 25°C (77°F)
- Classification: Nonmetallic

Like anything intriguing, I'm hard to pin down. I'm a Dr. Jekyll and Mr. Hyde element—essential to life, yet wickedly dangerous at the same time—a chameleon that appears in black, red, or white. I play a pivotal part in the DNA molecule and in the body, but I can be deadly. My white form ignites in air and even burns underwater! I can inflict terrible burns, and sadly I was used for that purpose in World War II. I am also a central element in sarin—a lethal nerve gas that has been used in a number of terrorist attacks.

Arguably my most important use is in fertilizers. I am also used in many foods as phosphoric acid (an acidifying agent). You can find me in any bottle of cola, which is why you can use this soft drink as a rust remover.

Date of discovery: 1669

Density	1.823 g/cm^3
Melting point	44.2°C (111.56°F)
Boiling point	277°C (530.6°F)

Phosphorus

33 **Arsenic**

The Nitrogen Elements

- Symbol: As
- Atomic number: 33
- Atomic weight: 74.922
- Color: Gray or yellow
- Standard state: Solid at 25°C (77°F)
- Classification: Metalloid

Make no mistake—I am a deadly element. A murderer's delight and a master of disguise to boot! One minute I'm a gray-colored metal, the next a yellow-colored nonmetal, and my furtive ability to hide with ease and avoid detection makes me a favorite choice of the poisoner.

Since I've got the properties of both a metal and a nonmetal, I'm known as a metalloid. I wreak havoc in developing countries, where industrial pollution allows me to sneak into the drinking water.

Contamination with me causes widespread health issues, but very small amounts of me are actually essential. You eat more of me than you'd care to know, with no ill effects—mostly in seafood such as shrimp.

Earliest known use: c. 1250

Density	5.727 g/cm^3
Melting point	817°C (1,502.6°F)
Boiling point	614°C (1,137.2°F)

Arsenic

51 **Antimony**

The Nitrogen Elements

- Symbol: Sb
- Atomic number: 51
- Atomic weight: 121.76
- Color: Silver-gray
- Standard state: Solid at 25°C (77°F)
- Classification: Metalloid

A curious and ancient metalloid, I am often found attached to other elements. Keep an eye out for me—although I'm used in mascara, I can induce violent vomiting and certain death. Like my buddy arsenic, I used to be popular among those with murder in mind. Today I'm more often used to make alloys and semiconductors.

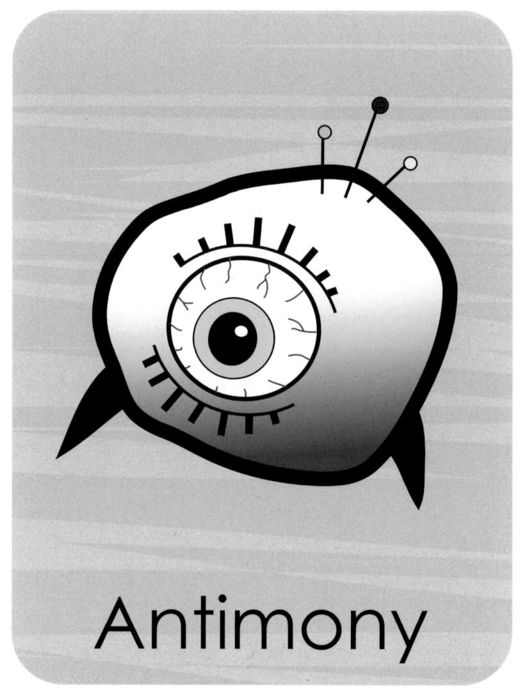

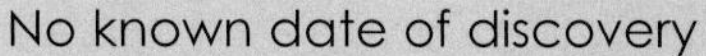

No known date of discovery

Sb

Density	6.697 g/cm^3
Melting point	630.63°C (1,167.13°F)
Boiling point	1,587°C (2,888.6°F)

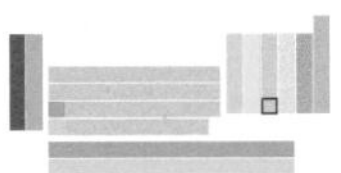

Bismuth 83

The Nitrogen Elements

- Symbol: Bi
- Atomic number: 83
- Atomic weight: 208.98
- Color: Silver-white
- Standard state: Solid at 25°C (77°F)
- Classification: Metalloid

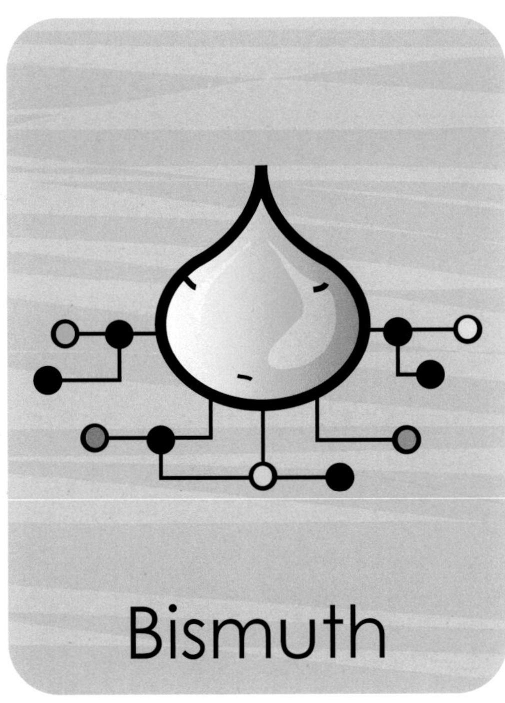

People tend to confuse me with tin or lead, which bugs me. I'm special too! I am the heaviest nonradioactive element. Others may decay to form more durable elements giving off radiation, but I'm stable. Because I can easily turn into a liquid, I am used as part of fire-alarm systems. When I melt in intense heat, this triggers the alarms and water sprinklers.

No known date of discovery

- Density 9.780 g/cm3
- Melting point 271.3°C (520.34°F)
- Boiling point 1,564°C (2,847.2°F)

Bi

CHAPTER 7

Group 16

The Oxygen Elements

In this neighborhood of the periodic table, the groups of elements are more like bunches of friends than family units. Nothing is truer for Group 16—it's a real mixed bag of solids, gases, nonmetals, metalloids, and even a radioactive metal—but the oxygen elements are a cosmopolitan crew that get involved in important industrial reactions and are vital to many life processes. They sport the unlikely name "the chalcogens," which means "ore formers," because in nature they are often found combined with metals.

8
O
OXYGEN

16
S
SULFUR

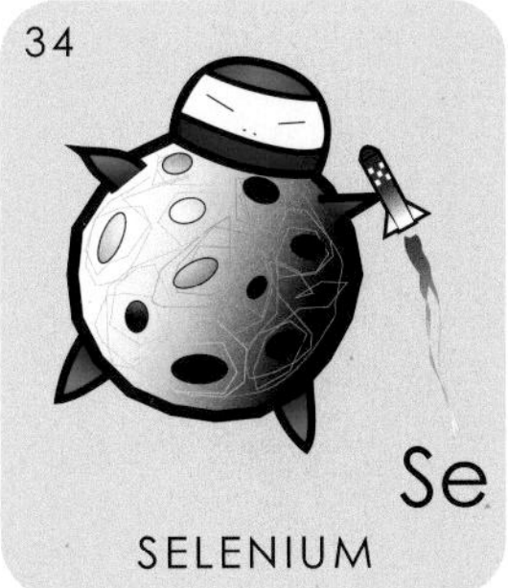
34
Se
SELENIUM

52
Te
TELLURIUM

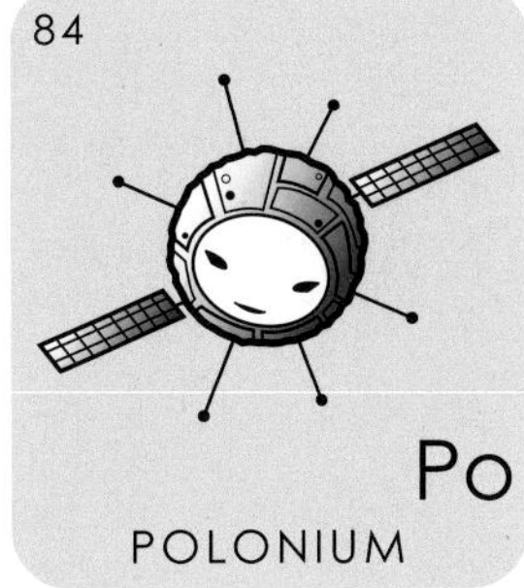
84
Po
POLONIUM

116
Lv
LIVERMORIUM

8 Oxygen

The Oxygen Elements

- Symbol: O
- Atomic number: 8
- Atomic weight: 15.999
- Color: None
- Standard state: Gas at 25°C (77°F)
- Classification: Nonmetallic

Quiet and unassuming, I'm colorless, odorless, and tasteless. Some say I lack personality, but they don't recognize true greatness. I am the powerhouse behind most chemical reactions on Earth. Without *me*, you die.

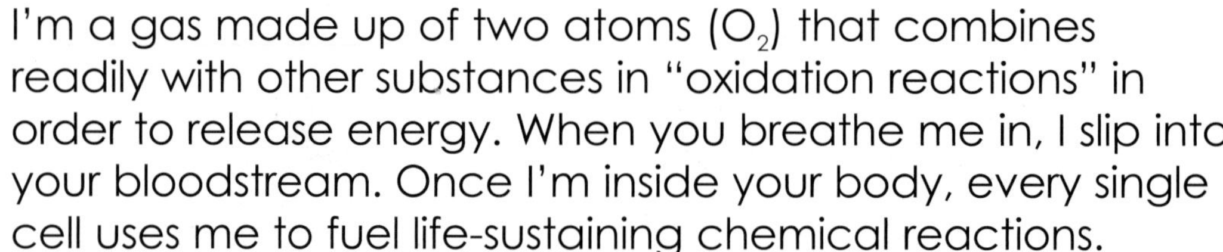

I'm a gas made up of two atoms (O_2) that combines readily with other substances in "oxidation reactions" in order to release energy. When you breathe me in, I slip into your bloodstream. Once I'm inside your body, every single cell uses me to fuel life-sustaining chemical reactions.

I am also found in teams of three atoms (O_3) as a gas known as ozone. When I take this form high up in the sky, I protect Earth from the Sun's harmful ultraviolet rays.

Date of discovery: 1774

- Density 1.308 g/l
- Melting point −218.3°C (−360.94°F)
- Boiling point −182.9°C (−297.22°F)

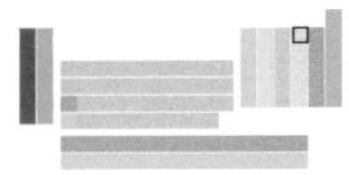

Oxygen

16 Sulfur

The Oxygen Elements

- Symbol: S
- Atomic number: 16
- Atomic weight: 32.065
- Color: Pale yellow
- Standard state: Solid at 25°C (77°F)
- Classification: Nonmetallic

Sweetly smiling and dressed in pale yellow, I look as harmless as a lemon tart, but I have a wicked side. . . . I am a fun-loving prankster that loves to unleash bad smells. My most vile whiffs include rotten eggs and foul skunky odors. But it's not really me—it's my compounds that stink—hydrogen sulfide (H_2S) is the most likely culprit.

I was once known as "brimstone" and featured in fiery descriptions of hell. This reputation probably comes from the fact that I ooze from the pores of active volcanoes. When exposed to oxygen and heated, I spontaneously combust with a bright and intense light. These qualities make me an important part of gunpowder. I also cause acid rain. I am an essential element in sulfuric acid—a chemical used to make a variety of other substances.

No known date of discovery

- Density 1.960 g/cm^3
- Melting point 115.21°C (239.38°F)
- Boiling point 444.72°C (832.5°F)

Sulfur

34 **Selenium**

The Oxygen Elements

- Symbol: Se
- Atomic number: 34
- Atomic weight: 78.96
- Color: Gray
- Standard state: Solid at 25°C (77°F)
- Classification: Nonmetallic

My name comes from the Greek word *selene*, meaning "moon"—I am a remote and mysterious element. A lack of me in your diet gives you Keshan disease, which causes heart muscle failure. But when animals eat me concentrated in plants such as vetch (a.k.a. "locoweed"), I make them stagger around as if they were drunk!

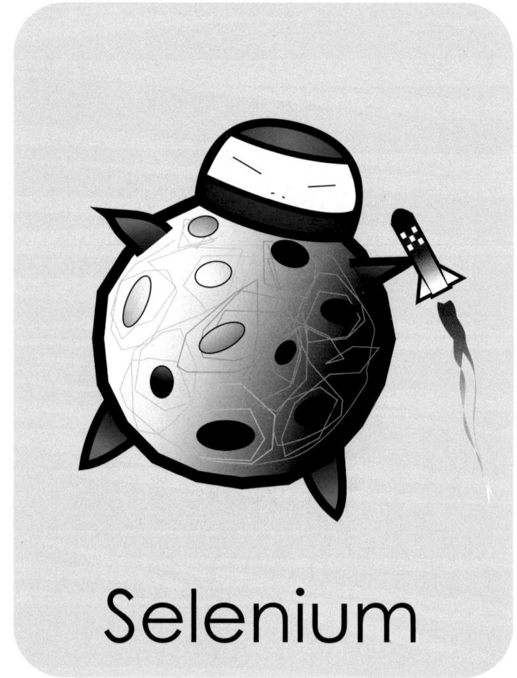

Date of discovery: 1817

Se

- Density 4.819 g/cm^3
- Melting point 221°C (429.8°F)
- Boiling point 685°C (1,265°F)

Tellurium 52

The Oxygen Elements

- Symbol: Te
- Atomic number: 52
- Atomic weight: 127.60
- Color: Silver-gray
- Standard state: Solid at 25°C (77°F)
- Classification: Semimetal

Although useful in electronics, I'm a real problem child. I've been a puzzle since day one, and identifying and classifying me has been a dizzying quandary. As a corrupting influence, I am without equal. I'm about the only compound that can touch the spotless gold. In the body I cause extremely bad breath, as well as horrible body odor.

Date of discovery: 1783

- Density 6.240 g/cm^3
- Melting point 449.51°C (841.12°F)
- Boiling point 988°C (1,810.4°F)

Te

CHAPTER 8

The Halogen Elements

Group 17

We're back in the family zone again, but this side of the periodic table is where the nonmetal elements live, separated from the metals to their left. The halogens are a close-knit group of lively, strongly colored nonmetals. They are a feisty bunch that will react violently with metals to form salts ("halogen" means "salt giver"). The elements at the top of Group 17 are yellow and green toxic gases, but as you move down through the group, things get progressively darker. . . .

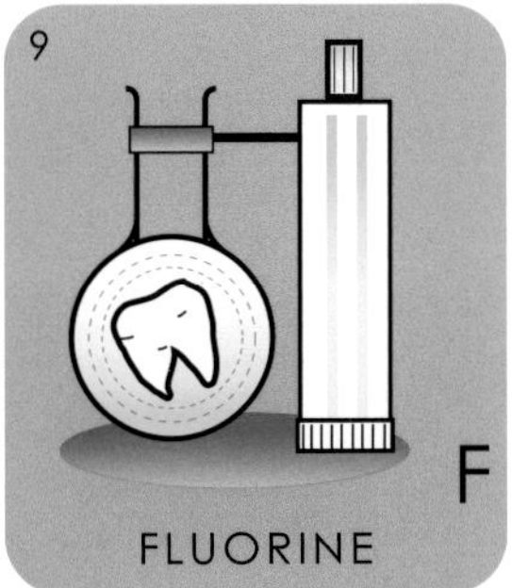
9
F
FLUORINE

17
Cl
CHLORINE

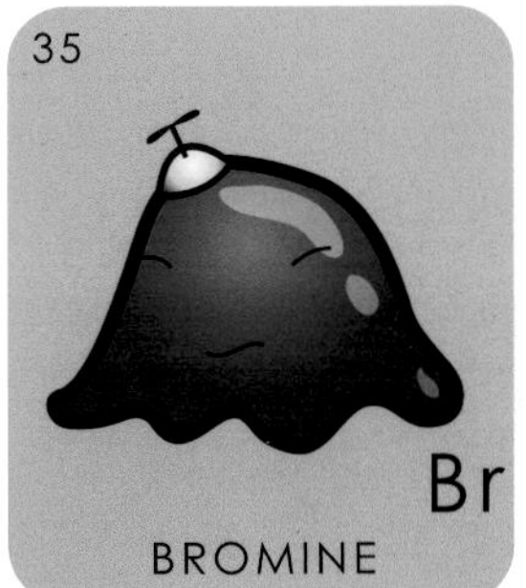
35
Br
BROMINE

53
I
IODINE

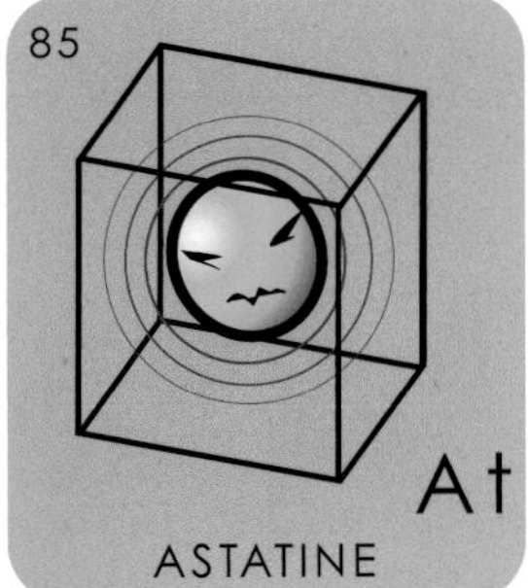
85
At
ASTATINE

117
Uus
ELEMENT 117

9 Fluorine

The Halogen Elements

- Symbol: F
- Atomic number: 9
- Atomic weight: 18.998
- Color: Pale yellow-green
- Standard state: Gas at 25°C (77°F)
- Classification: Nonmetallic

I'm a doer—a lively package set off by the perfect Hollywood smile. I am added to drinking water to help protect your teeth, and I form lots of really useful compounds—such as Teflon®, the famous nonstick coating. Running through all of the wonderful things I do is a competitive streak. I am superreactive, and I will take an electron from almost any atom or molecule in order to complete my set. This is just one of the reasons why I'm so usable and form so many nifty compounds.

The only blot on my record is my involvement with CFCs (chlorofluorocarbons)—the compounds that have done so much damage to Earth's ozone layer. I don't like to talk about it. My invasive choking smell signals my true toxic nature. So, be warned!

Date of discovery: 1886

- Density 1.553 g/l
- Melting point −219.62°C (−363.32°F)
- Boiling point −188.12°C (−306.62°F)

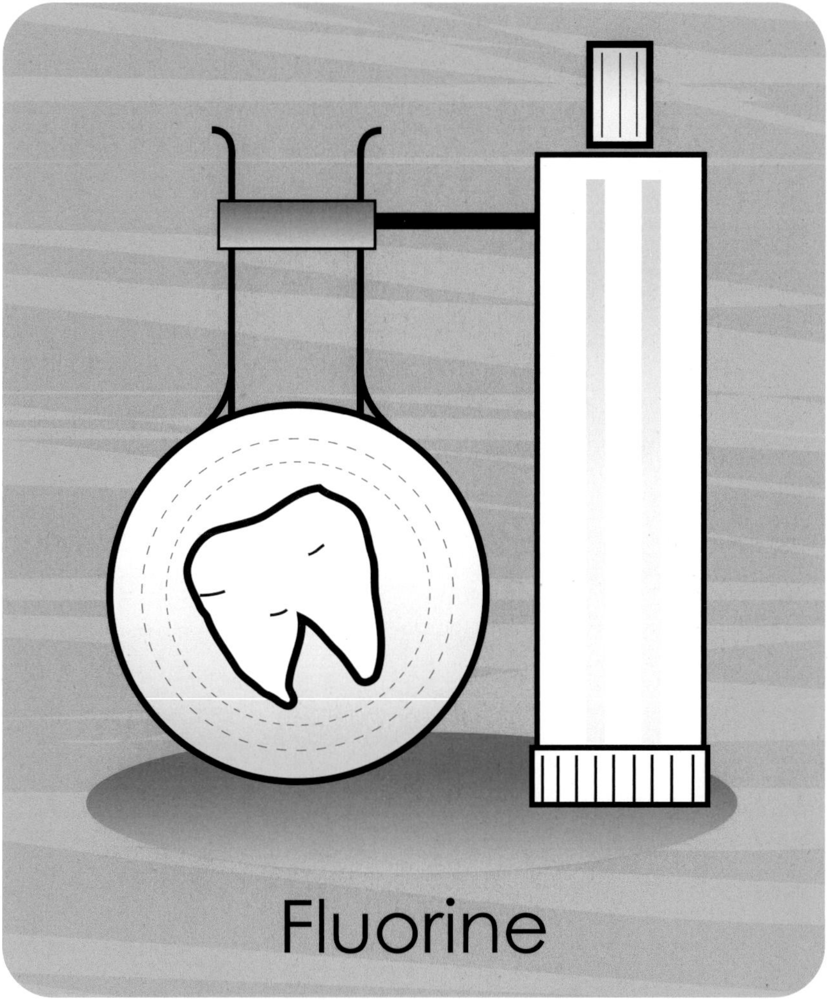

Fluorine

17 Chlorine

The Halogen Elements

- Symbol: Cl
- Atomic number: 17
- Atomic weight: 35.453
- Color: Green
- Standard state: Gas at 25°C (77°F)
- Classification: Nonmetallic

You've gotta give me some respect! I'm a mean, green, killing machine. One of the halogen gang, I'm a toxic gas with a horrible history. I first became a terrifying chemical weapon during World War I, when my sinister, choking fumes killed thousands of people. I'm even bad enough to battle bacteria in the toilet bowl! But I can also keep you safe from waterborne diseases such as cholera and typhoid fever. Adding small amounts of me to drinking water supplies has saved millions of people's lives.

Usually obtained from common salt, you'll find me in all sorts of places, from saltshakers to swimming pools (where I keep the water bacteria-free). I have also been used as an especially un-environmentally friendly pesticide called DDT and am associated with CFCs (see Fluorine).

Date of discovery: 1774

- Density 2.898 g/l
- Melting point −101.5°C (−150.7°F)
- Boiling point −34.04°C (−29.27°F)

Chlorine

35 Bromine

The Halogen Elements

- Symbol: Br
- Atomic number: 35
- Atomic weight: 79.904
- Color: Orangish-brown
- Standard state: Liquid at 25°C (77°
- Classification: Nonmetallic

I am a regal element with a long history. One of only two liquids in the periodic table (the other is mercury), I was used in the royal dye of the ancient Roman Empire—"Tyrian purple." Made from crushed seashells, emperors and members of the imperial family wore me proudly to show everyone else how important they were.

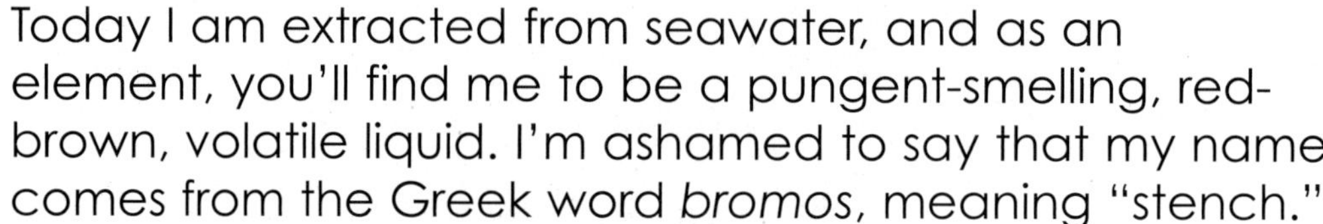

Today I am extracted from seawater, and as an element, you'll find me to be a pungent-smelling, red-brown, volatile liquid. I'm ashamed to say that my name comes from the Greek word *bromos*, meaning "stench."

Until recently, doctors used my salts to suppress mental activity in disturbed patients, but not anymore, since their toxic nature has been revealed.

Date of discovery: 1826

- Density: 3.1028 g/cm^3
- Melting point: −7.3°C (18.9°F)
- Boiling point: 59°C (138.2°F)

Br

Bromine

53 Iodine

The Halogen Elements

- Symbol: I
- Atomic number: 53
- Atomic weight: 126.90
- Color: Shiny black
- Standard state: Solid at 25°C (77°F)
- Classification: Nonmetallic

Appearances can be deceiving. I am a shiny black solid, but at room temperature I often change into a purplish gas—without stopping to become liquid. That's called sublimation.

You'll almost never see me alone—I hang out in pairs as a gas (I_2). I am deadly to bacteria when I'm in a solution. I am a yellow-brown liquid that stings like heck when it gets dabbed onto a cut (although this may be the fault of the liquid alcohol). My antiseptic powers are so good that I'm used to clean up inside the body after surgery.

I've been sneaking into people's diets for many years disguised in table salt, but that's a good thing—I help eliminate the horrible swellings of the neck that used to affect people who didn't have enough of me inside their bodies.

Date of discovery: 1811

- Density: 4.940 g/cm^3
- Melting point: 113.7°C (236.66°F)
- Boiling point: 184.3°C (363.74°F)

Iodine

CHAPTER 9

The Noble Gases

Group 18

The far right of the table is the classy neighborhood, for here lives the periodic table's royal family—the so-called "noble gases." This group is largely resistant to chemical reactions, seemingly above mixing or slumming it with the rest of the elements. They were once called the "inert gases," meaning completely unreactive, but this isn't entirely true—some of them have been caught in clandestine clinches with other elements. They're not even that rare either—we now know that they all float around in the atmosphere, alone and aloof.

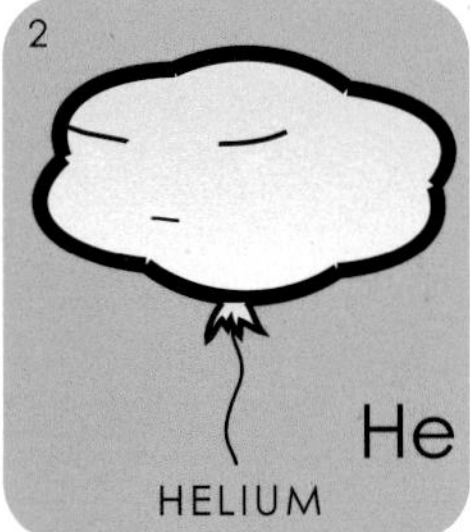
2
He
HELIUM

10
Ne
NEON

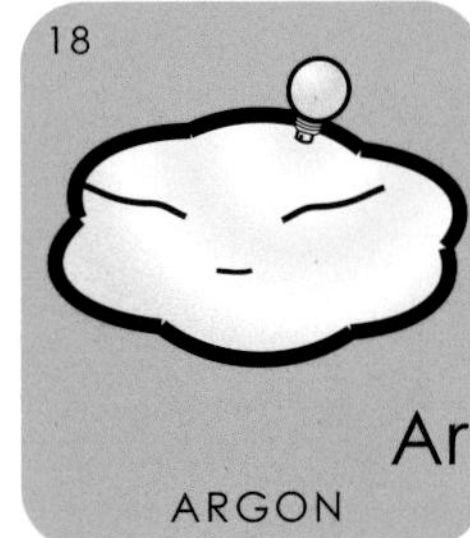
18
Ar
ARGON

36
Kr
KRYPTON

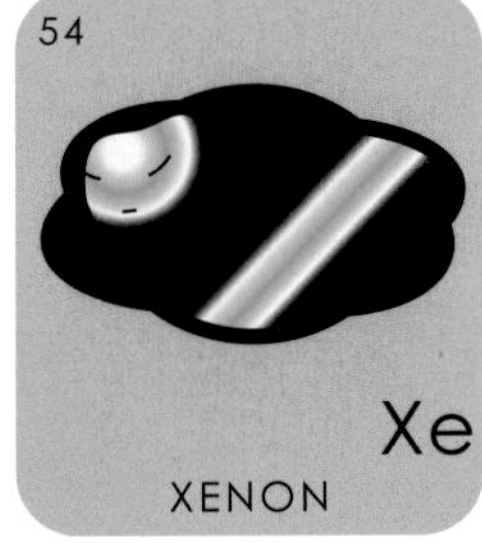
54
Xe
XENON

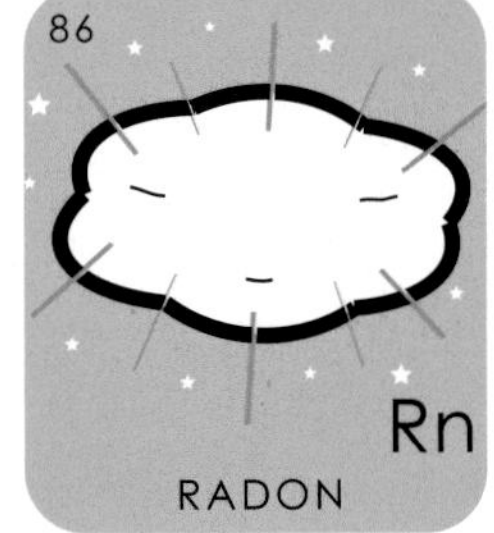
86
Rn
RADON

118
Uuo
ELEMENT 118

2 Helium

The Noble Gases

- Symbol: He
- Atomic number: 2
- Atomic weight: 4.0026
- Color: None
- Standard state: Gas at 25°C (77°F)
- Classification: Nonmetallic

I prefer my own company, thank you very much. Some call me aloof, but I'm happy not to mix with the riffraff of the periodic table. I am a "noble" gas—the very first. I am completely inert, with no color, taste, or smell. I am also known as a party prankster. Gulp me from a birthday balloon, and your voice will get all squeaky!

I am produced in massive stars like the Sun, where four hydrogen atoms fuse together, releasing enormous amounts of energy. On Earth, my nucleus is one of the products of radioactive decay—the alpha particle.

My main uses are in weather balloons and airships—which need my lofty, lighter-than-air properties—and in welding, which requires an inert, unreactive atmosphere.

Date of discovery: 1895

- Density: 0.164 g/l
- Melting point: −272.2°C (−457.96°F)
- Boiling point: −268.93°C (−452.07°F)

Helium

10 Neon

The Noble Gases

- Symbol: Ne
- Atomic number: 10
- Atomic weight: 20.18
- Color: None
- Standard state: Gas at 25°C (77°F)
- Classification: Nonmetallic

I must be the funkiest element around. My name is derived from the Greek word *neos*, which means "new." (Maybe any new element could have been christened this way, but I think it suits me very well.) Things really get going when I become excited by electrical energy—my electrons zap and zing and make me emit bright, brilliant, and stunningly colored red light. When other elements are stirred into the mix, I can produce all the colors of the rainbow. This is how neon lights are made.

Even though I am found in something as common as air, I am a member of the periodic table's aristocracy—the noble gases. I keep myself to myself. I am a colorless, odorless, and tasteless gas, and there is virtually nothing that I will react with.

Date of discovery: 1898

- Density 0.825 g/l
- Melting point −248.59°C (−415.46°F)
- Boiling point −246.08°C (−410.94°F)

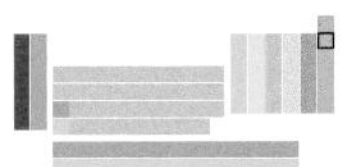

Neon

18 **Argon**

The Noble Gases

- Symbol: Ar
- Atomic number: 18
- Atomic weight: 39.948
- Color: None
- Standard state: Gas at 25°C (77°F)
- Classification: Nonmetallic

Bone idle and basically lazy, I'm totally lackluster—an odorless, colorless, and tasteless gas, but don't call me a good-for-nothing. I'm renowned for my unwillingness and inability to react with anything at all! This can be a good thing—I am used as an "inert atmosphere" in potentially dangerous jobs, such as arc welding, when oxygen must be excluded in order to avoid explosions. I am also sometimes used in lightbulbs. You can even find me between the panes of some windows because I am such a poor conductor of heat.

As the third most abundant gas in Earth's atmosphere, I'm extracted from liquid air. Because I am produced when the radioactive isotope potassium-40 decays, my presence in the atmosphere is increasing with time.

Date of discovery: 1894

- Density 1.633 g/l
- Melting point −189.3°C (−308.74°F)
- Boiling point −185.8°C (−302.44°F)

Argon

36 Krypton

■ The Noble Gases

- Symbol: Kr
- Atomic number: 36
- Atomic weight: 83.798
- Color: None
- Standard state: Gas at 25°C (77°F)
- Classification: Nonmetallic

I'm elusive to say the least! My name, from the Greek *kryptos*, means "hidden," and it is aptly chosen. I'm almost completely unreactive, colorless, odorless, and tasteless, and I'm only present in the atmosphere in vanishingly small amounts. Don't confuse me with the fictional home planet of Superman and the source of his nemesis—kryptonite!

Date of discovery: 1898

Kr

Density	3.425 g/l
Melting point	–157.36°C (–251.25°F)
Boiling point	–153.22°C (–243.8°F)

Radon 86

The Noble Gases

- Symbol: Rn
- Atomic number: 86
- Atomic weight: 222.02
- Color: None
- Standard state: Gas at 25°C (77°F)
- Classification: Nonmetallic

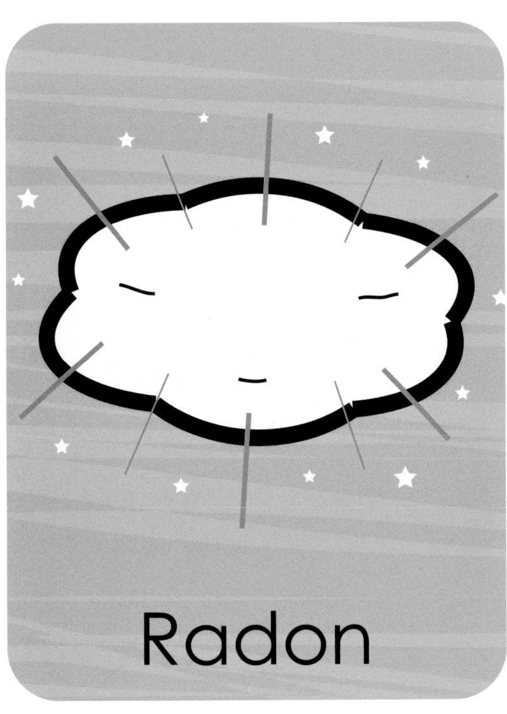

Like my other "noble" family members, I'm almost completely immune to chemical reactions, but I'm a much more sparky character than the rest. I give off harmful radioactive alpha particles, and, since I occur in granite, there is a concern that I may build up inside houses in granitic areas and pose a risk of lung cancer.

Date of discovery: 1900

- Density 9.074 g/l
- Melting point −71°C (−95.8°F)
- Boiling point −61.7°C (−79.06°F)

Rn

CHAPTER 10
The Lanthanides and Actinides

Removed from the main body of the periodic table, the lanthanides and actinides are outcasts. Sometimes called the "f-block" elements, they are a loosely grouped bunch of misfits. The lanthanides are naturally occurring heavy metals, used to date the rocks from outer space and widely utilized in lasers. The actinides are all dangerously radioactive elements. Only two of them are naturally occurring—the rest are produced in nuclear reactors and particle accelerators and decay (break down) in the blink of an eye.

57 La LANTHANUM

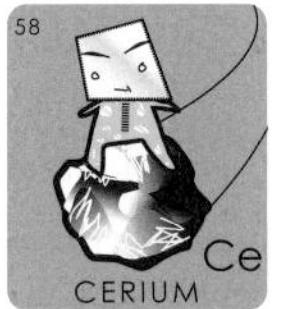
58 Ce CERIUM

59 Pr PRASEODYMIUM

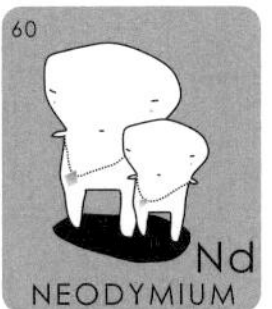
60 Nd NEODYMIUM

61 Pm PROMETHIUM

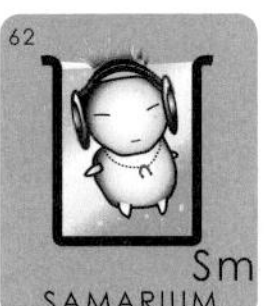
62 Sm SAMARIUM

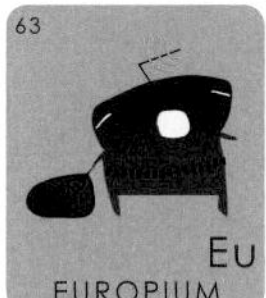
63 Eu EUROPIUM

64 Gd GADOLINIUM

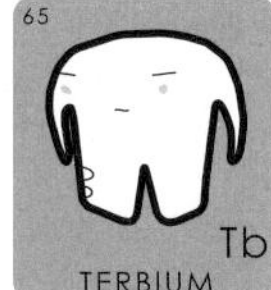
65 Tb TERBIUM

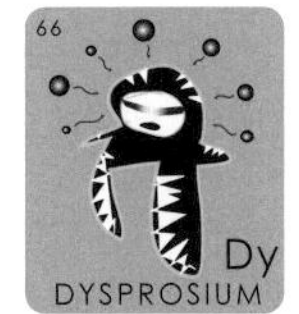
66 Dy DYSPROSIUM

67 Ho HOLMIUM

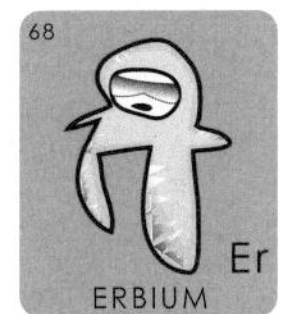
68 Er ERBIUM

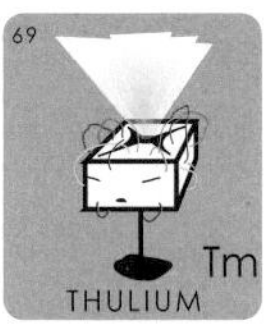
69 Tm THULIUM

70 Yb YTTERBIUM

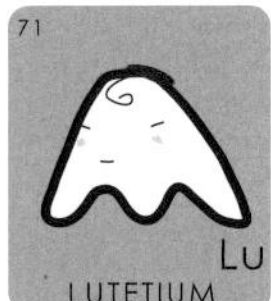
71 Lu LUTETIUM

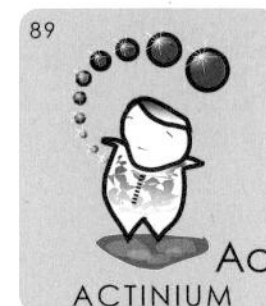
89 Ac ACTINIUM

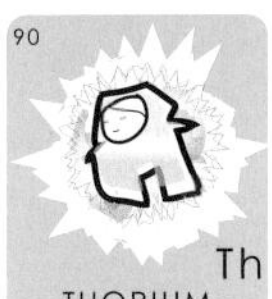
90 Th THORIUM

91 Pa PROTACTINIUM

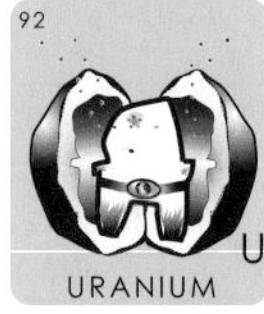
92 U URANIUM

93 Np NEPTUNIUM

94 Pu PLUTONIUM

95 Am AMERICIUM

96 Cm CURIUM

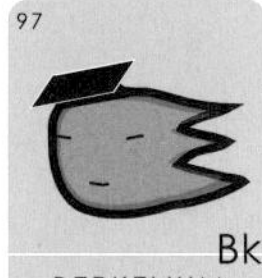
97 Bk BERKELIUM

98 Cf CALIFORNIUM

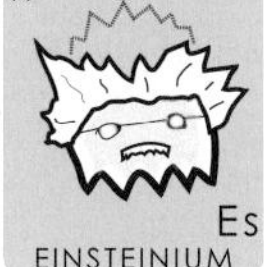
99 Es EINSTEINIUM

100 Fm FERMIUM

101 Md MENDELEVIUM

102 No NOBELIUM

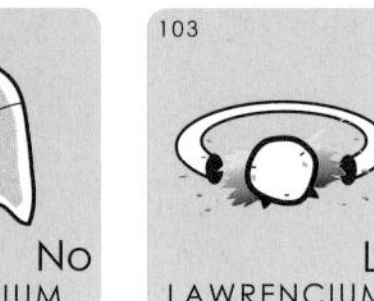
103 Lr LAWRENCIUM

92 Uranium

The Lanthanides and Actinides

- Symbol: U
- Atomic number: 92
- Atomic weight: 238.03
- Color: Gray
- Standard state: Solid at 25°C (77°F)
- Classification: Metallic

I am a force of nature—one of the most powerful elements and the one with the greatest impact on history. My secret lies within my nucleus, and the key is simple but deadly. Take a neutron and fire it at my unstable, radioactive form (atomic number 235). My nucleus splits apart with a roar of energy, firing neutrons in all directions. These go on to split other nuclei as I allow the chain reaction to rip me apart!

When this mighty reaction (called nuclear fission) is controlled in nuclear reactors, it can be used to generate power, but pack me into a bomb, and I can cause chaos. I can flatten whole cities. In 1945 an atomic bomb made out of me was dropped on Hiroshima, Japan, with horrific results—signaling the start of the Atomic Age.

Date of discovery: 1789

- Density 19.050 g/cm^3
- Melting point 1,132.2°C (2,069.96°F)
- Boiling point 3,927°C (7,100.6°F)

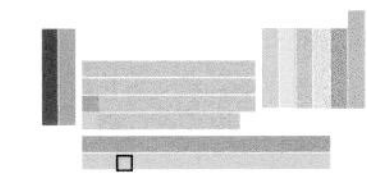

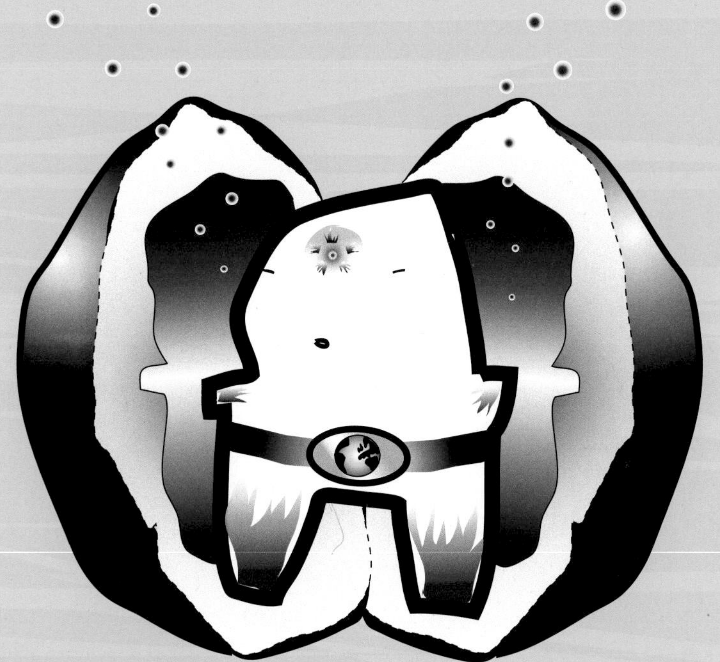

Uranium

94 **Plutonium**

The Lanthanides and Actinides

- Symbol: Pu
- Atomic number: 94
- Atomic weight: 244.06
- Color: Silver-white
- Standard state: Solid at 25°C (77°F)
- Classification: Metallic

Unlike that Disney dog, life ain't no cartoon for me—I'm deadly serious. Born in Berkeley, California, in 1941, I was made by nuclear scientists, who named me after the dwarf planet, Pluto. My nucleus was soon the center of attention. In August 1945 a nuclear bomb made from my "239" isotope was dropped on the Japanese city of Nagasaki. It killed or injured close to 200,000 people and effectively ended World War II.

Although I'm dull to look at, inside I'm hot stuff. A lump of me radiates heat because of the enormous amount of radioactive alpha particles that I release. I'm still closely guarded because of my bomb-making potential, but I can be used for peaceful purposes too. I am a by-product of nuclear power plants.

Date of discovery: 1940

- Density 19.816 g/cm^3
- Melting point 639.4°C (1,182.9°F)
- Boiling point 3,230°C (5,846°F)

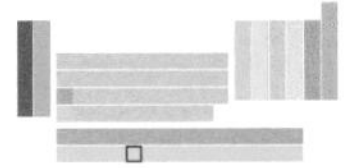

Plutonium

CHAPTER 11

The Superheavies

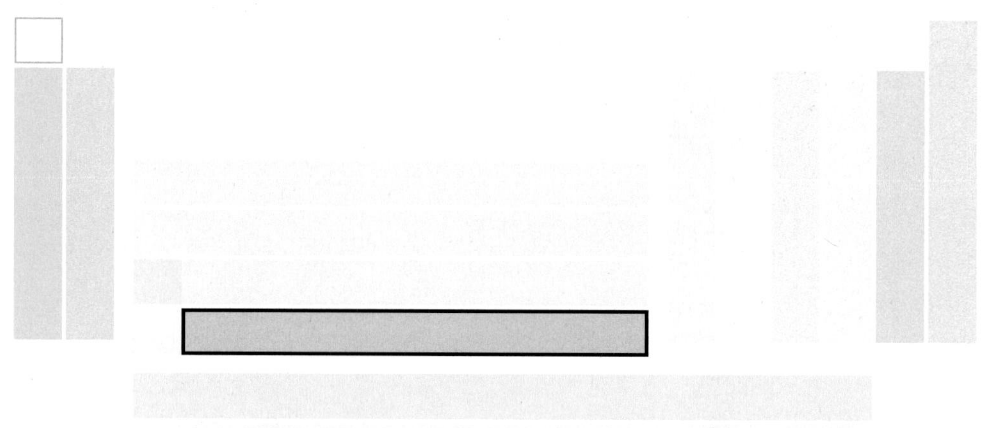

This group is totally "out there." Here at the far reaches of the periodic table live elements with atomic numbers greater than 103. These superheavy substances have all been artificially created in the lab, so most of them have only ever existed in minuscule amounts. Every single one is extremely radioactive and decays incredibly quickly. Many labs all around the world lay claim to having been the first to produce these elements, so there is always a great deal of healthy argument about what each element should be called.

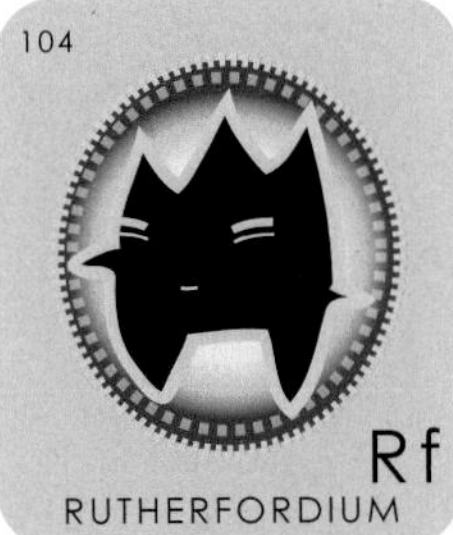
104
Rf
RUTHERFORDIUM

105
Db
DUBNIUM

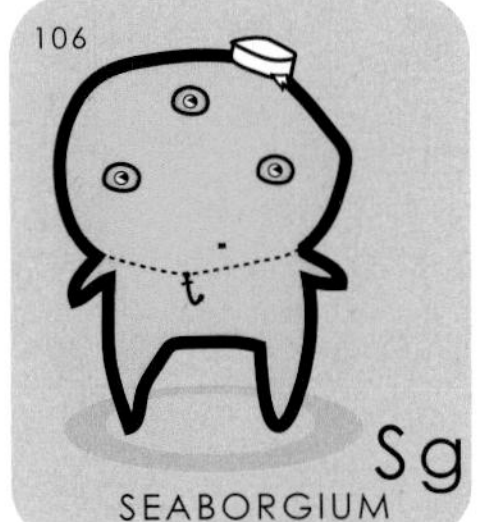
106
Sg
SEABORGIUM

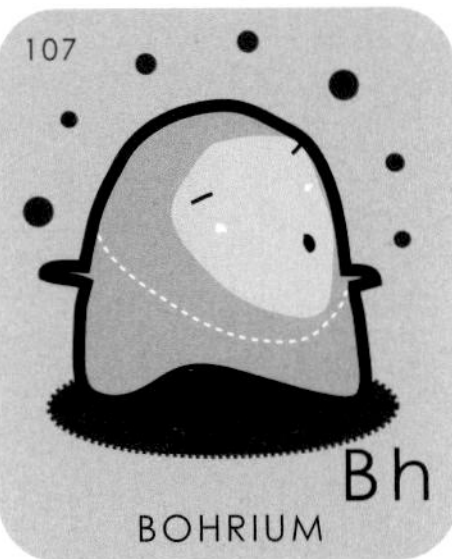
107
Bh
BOHRIUM

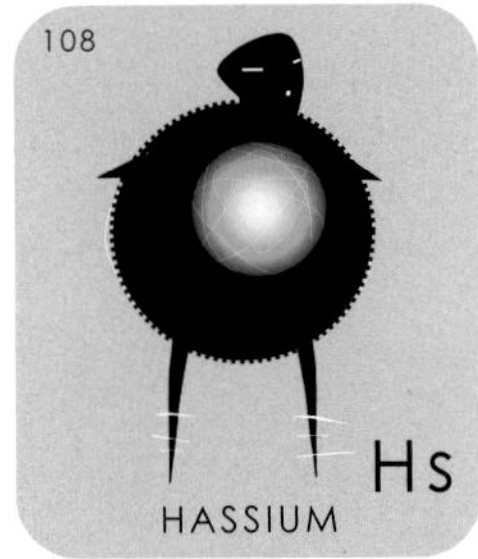
108
Hs
HASSIUM

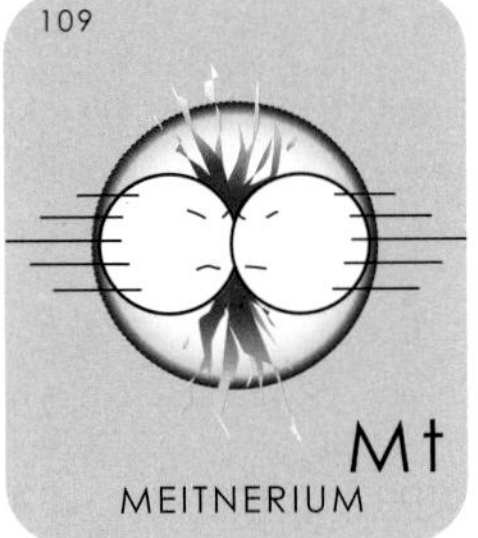
109
Mt
MEITNERIUM

110
Ds
DARMSTADTIUM

111
Rg
ROENTGENIUM

112
Cn
COPERNICIUM

INDEX

GLOSSARY

Alchemy Medieval attempts to convert base metals into gold.
Alloy A mixture of metals.
Alpha particle A positively charged particle (a helium nucleus) given off during some types of radioactive decay.
Atom The fundamental building block of all matter.
Beta particle A negatively charged particle (an electron) given off during some types of radioactive decay.
Catalyst A substance that speeds up a chemical reaction.
Compound A substance created by the chemical bonding of elements.
Electron A subatomic particle with a negative charge.
Element A substance that cannot be further broken down by chemical reactions.
Gamma ray High-energy electromagnetic radiation given off by some nuclei.
Group A vertical column of elements on the periodic table. These elements often have closely related properties.
Ion A charged particle formed when an atom loses or gains electrons.
Ionization The process of producing ions.
Isotope Atoms of the same element that have the same number of protons and electrons but differing numbers of neutrons.
Neutron A subatomic particle with a neutral charge.
Nucleus The center of an atom where protons and neutrons are found.
Oxide A compound of one element with oxygen.
Particle accelerator A machine that can produce new elements by colliding charged particles at high speeds.
Period A horizontal row of elements on the periodic table.
Proton A subatomic particle with a positive charge.
Radioactivity The spontaneous disintegration of certain nuclei accompanied by the emission of alpha, beta, or gamma radiation.
Salts Compounds formed when the hydrogen ions in an acid are replaced by metal ions or other positive ions.